CW00348274

NOT VERY
INTELLIGENT
DESIGN
TOO
-
PLANET EARTH

NOT VERY INTELLIGENT DESIGN TOO

-

PLANET EARTH
A Perfect Place for Human Life?

by
Neel Ingman

ABOUT THE AUTHOR

Neel Ingman is an independent blogger who is almost universally unknown for publishing his conversations with God and the Pope, and other stuff at neelingman.com.

He occasionally spends too much time Tweeting about random stuff under the handle @NeelIngman.

Neel's brother, Mark Ingman, was originally going to be co-author of this work but Neel and Mark reached a point where they could no longer collaborate or even regard each other as almost equals.

This unfortunate situation was brought about by a faulty front wheel on an e-scooter which caused Mark to suffer the ignominy of having his life squelched out under the wheels of a bright yellow Hummer H2.

Neel will miss him terribly, except for his never-ending hyper-critical comments about everything, which will not be missed by anyone.

Version 1.0

First Publication, 2020

Palaceno House
Auckland
New Zealand

Not Very Intelligent Design Too : Planet Earth, A Perfect Place for Human Life?

ISBN   978-0-473-47396-9   (Softcover)
ISBN   978-0-473-47397-6   (Epub)
ISBN   978-0-473-47398-3   (Kindle)
ISBN   978-0-473-47399-0   (PDF)
ISBN   978-0-473-47400-3   (iBook)

neelingman.com

NotVeryIntelligentDesign.com

kneelingman.com

Available from Amazon.com

CONTENTS

TRIGGER WARNING

This book was triggered by the book Not Very Intelligent Design. It's not the only thing that was triggered by that book. Some persons of faith were triggered to write scathing reviews about it, saying it was unscientific, shallow, subjective, and worst of all, vulgar.

Heads up, creationists. This one is too. Even worse, it lurches off into hyperbole and straight out fiction.

Hopefully it's also funny and honest. At least more intellectually honest than a creationist who claims to be offended by the idea of something being unscientific.

If you're the sort of person who gets angry when your beliefs are challenged or threatened by simple, easy to comprehend concepts that your faith can't deal with, don't read this book. If language sometimes used by politicians upsets your delicate sensibilities, don't read this book. If you're perturbed by observations regarding serious or scientific matters that are neither serious nor scientific, don't read this book.

You've been warned. To go ahead and read it, perhaps using it as a tool for self-flagellation, is not only unwise, it may also lead you unto the temptation of bearing false witness against it for being exactly what it purports to be. Seriously, if you're any of the above types, don't read it. It's not for you. You'll hate it.

To everybody else, happy reading. I hope you enjoy it.

INTRODUCTION

Human migration is as old as humanity itself. People have always been motivated to try to improve their lives, often by trying to find a better place to live. Places can be too hot, too cold, too windy, too dry, too wet or too conducive to saber-toothed tigers.

In the modern world people also get on the move for holiday purposes. Which indicates that there are nicer places to be than the place where you live. Nobody leaves a nice place to go for a holiday in a dump, although most camping grounds, theme parks and the Kuta zone of Bali are good evidence that a "nice place" is a highly subjective concept. Holiday congestion is caused by millions of people simultaneously travelling to somewhere nicer than the place they live in order to try to have a better time than they could have by staying at home. Thousands of grumpy dads would disagree.

It has been said that all problems are problems of geography. This is meant to be a humorous way of saying that if people are making your life difficult, there's a good chance that problem can be solved by going elsewhere. But if the problem actually is the geography, the physical characteristics of the location itself, then you have an even better chance of solving the problem by packing your bags.

Many thousands of people get on the move in planes, trains, automobiles, and pedestrian caravans, every single day. If you live in an excellent environment why would you pack up your family and move thousands of miles in the hope of finding somewhere better?

Which brings us to the premise of this book. Was the earth designed and fine-tuned over the course of six days specifically for the benefit of homo sapiens?

Those who believe that humans were created by an intelligent designer would say, of course it was. They think the whole universe was designed and fine-tuned specifically for our benefit, for us to utilize and exploit. (Us in this case usually meaning fellow members of our own particular faith tribe.) But is there any evidence for that?

Rather than going into theories, scientific or otherwise, about the origin and history of the planet, this book will take a look at exactly what's here now. Is this planet a perfectly designed place for human existence or is it merely a place that's good enough to serve the purpose?

"Lovely day today." Such expressions are voiced all over the world millions of times every day. Except when the weather's crap. Which, at any given moment it is, in most places.

If every day were lovely, or even most days, a lovely day wouldn't be worth a mention. The only people that say "lovely day" in Southern California are tourists. For locals it's redundant.

There are quite a few places where the weather's good most of the time. We know this because we pay thousands of dollars to go there for two weeks to bask in the comfort of good weather, weather that's so good it actually makes our bodies feel good all the way through. Then we return to live in places that make our bodies feel not so good. The effect is amplified as we age. There's nothing like a damp chill to induce serious pain in the joints of anyone with a few decades on the clock.

If this planet was designed specifically for humans, why is it that at any given moment so much of it is unpleasant, inhospitable or downright life-threatening? For example, the polar regions, the mountains, the deserts, the jungles (which won't be a problem for much longer as we're getting rid of them fairly rapidly), the winter half of the planet and anywhere the wind's blowing in double digits. In other words, most places, or bloody near the whole planet, most of the time.

The premise of this book is that a perfect environment for humans would be one where we could comfortably live without a requirement for clothing or buildings to protect us from the elements. We may decide we'd prefer to have those things, but needing them to survive indicates the environment is not perfect for the human body.

If we colonize Mars one day, there may be people who'll prefer to live there, but that wouldn't mean that Mars could be regarded as a good environment for human habitation, even for those who like the idea.

There are many people who say they prefer colder climates and don't ever enjoy temperatures above, say, 22°C (72°F). If that's how you feel, that's fine, just think of England, and apply your own pinch of salt where necessary. There's a section in the conclusion with an adjusted result that takes that temperature preference into account. So there's something for everybody to look forward to.

While almost all of the events in this book take place on planet earth, some of them take place in one of the nearby alternate universe versions of planet earth.

OUR PLACE IN SPACE AND TIME

Where the fuck are we?

The centre of the universe of course. One of the first things that infants learn is that they possess the power to summon food and comfort just by making a noise. They scream, and the thing they desire magically arrives before they have any real idea of what on earth's going on. Accordingly, it takes quite a while for human infants to begin to accept the idea that we, as young children, are not the centre of the universe.

As we grow towards adulthood, most of us learn that we are but one of many, and there's nothing intrinsically special about us, even though every one of us is a unique individual. We all learn this at a different rate, just as we eventually learn that becoming an actual adult who understands how most things work is definitely not a given. But we muddle on regardless.

Some people have such trouble with growing up, and especially the notion that they're not special, that they buy into a huge fantasy-based system in which they are indeed at the centre of the universe in every possible way. Including the idea that the creator of the universe knows everything about them and cares about them as an individual. Some of them pray, a lot, to help them sustain their belief. They also believe that their prayers will be heard and answered, even though there's never been any real evidence to support that ever having happened.

The story goes that the creator created the whole universe specifically to accommodate the human animal, and so of course we are at the very centre of the space-time system. The universe is in fact, or at least as far as we know, so damn big that we have no idea how close we are to the centre, or if there even is a centre. If it's infinitely big then the centre is everywhere and nowhere baby, that's where it's at. Our sun is shining somewhere in a vast space-time continuum with a high ho silver lining.

It's probably easier to think of it like being on a small boat in an ocean, with no land in sight. It seems like you're in the middle because it looks the same in all directions, but you may be just a few miles from shore in one direction and thousands of miles from shore in others.

As far as space goes, we may be somewhere near the centre of the universe, but the chances of that are slim, so it's smarter to just accept that we don't know. Which brings us to...

When the fuck are we?

What is our place in time? Once again it sort of feels like we're in the middle. Time stretches away behind us so far that it's beyond imagination how long everything's been here, and even for those who accept the scientific consensus that planet earth has existed for four and a half billion years, what the hell does that even mean, and how is it any different from forever?

Try this quick mental exercise. Think about what forty million years is like. Now try to imagine four billion years. Now try eight million years. And finally have a go at imagining forever. Without comparing them to each other, is it possible to imagine any difference between them at all, or to describe them in any way that would give some idea of what any of them are like?

How much time lies ahead is equally opaque. So it doesn't seem unreasonable to say that we're right in the middle of time and space. So we must be special.

Although, given what we know about the universe, every point in time, except for that first sixty-four thousandth of a second and a few million years after that, would likely feel the same, and so would every location.

Except for Perth, Australia. Perth does feel like it's on the edge, as far away from everywhere and everything as it's possible to be, and you don't even have to go down to the sea to get that feeling. In fact, it's a good idea not to go down to Cottesloe Beach in the afternoon as the Fremantle Doctor's likely to whip sand into your eyes with such velocity that it'll blind you, and then it'll tear your ears off as you turn away. Apart from that, and the flies, it's really lovely.

Closing in by a few orders of magnitude, we know, very accurately, our place in the sun, meaning our location in this particular solar system. We know this so accurately that we can launch rockets and land them on the moon. And send them to other planets when we think up a reason to do so.

We are at exactly the right distance from our sun to be not too hot, and not too cold. This is known as the Goldilocks Zone. Meaning a perfect place for humans to live. A place where water, which we're mostly made of, naturally exists as a liquid, which is good, because we need the water in our bodies to remain in liquid form so that we stay flexible.

But not all of our planet is always at a temperature where water is liquid. Sometimes, in some places, it's cold enough for water to be ice, which is not good, because if the water in our bodies turns to ice it's really hard to walk and talk and breath and do yoga. Actually impossible. And your fingers snap off. Although they do give you a bit of warning by turning black first.

If water gets too hot, it boils. Which is also not good inside a human being. Lobsters know the danger of boiling water better than most humans. Actually that's not true at all. Lobsters generally don't have any idea about it because they don't have the opportunity to pass the knowledge on to their offspring until it's way too late to do so. Which is why it'll continue to be easy to keep catching them and boiling them. At least until we've eaten most of them.

Many people think it's cruel to boil lobsters because of the pain involved. They say the same thing about bricking camels. But boiling lobsters doesn't hurt unless one of the rubber bands snaps and they grab you by the pinky. Or by the nose if you're a cartoon character.

Our place in the solar system is exactly in the zone where we can live and thrive. There are other planets in other solar systems that are the right temperature, but they're so far away we don't know very much about them. Yet. Their existence is more likely to be true than not, because of the size of the universe. In fact, if the universe is infinitely large then not only will there be other planets similar to this one, there'll be other planets exactly the same. Right down to your annoying neighbors. Infinity is a very difficult concept to grasp and is thankfully beyond the scope of whatever this book's meant to be.

So that's the temperature thing lightly touched upon, but what about other stuff? Such as the air that we breath?

THE "O" ZONE

O is for oxygen. And the O Zone is everywhere that oxygen freely exists as a gas.

We talk about oxygen because that's the gas that we mostly seem to need, even though the atmosphere is four fifths nitrogen and only one fifth oxygen. There's a tiny bit of other stuff, but not enough to worry about. Actually there's plenty to worry about, but pollution and climate change are not what this book's concerned with.

Fortunately for humans, we can inhale and thrive on the exact mixture of gases that exists in earth's atmosphere. Other creatures are also fortunate in the same way. The other thing that seems fortunate is that this breathable gas is available everywhere we go, except for Machu Picchu, Mt Everest and cities with too much stink in the air from diesel and petrol engines. We haven't polluted Machu Picchu and Mt Everest yet, because there's not enough oxygen there for diesel engines to run very well.

The thing that's worth noting about the O Zone is that it's very thin. The ozone layer over Antarctica is also very thin, but that's not the O Zone layer we're talking about here. Earth's atmosphere hugs the ground so tightly that it doesn't properly go all the way to the top of Mt Everest, as previously mentioned. Which is why breathing gets difficult. And that might matter if it wasn't also so cold and uncomfortable that only crazy fools would ever go up there.

The very thin, breathable bit of the atmosphere is thinner than an egg shell, relatively speaking. It's about 12km, or 7.5 miles thick, compared to earth's diameter of 12,700 km (7,900 miles). Like a coat of paint on a basketball. The part of the world that's available for mankind to occupy is within this thin layer and is pretty much 2 dimensional, or flat, for all big picture purposes. Except when it comes to falling. If you're in a plane that falls out of the sky, it really won't matter whether you listened to the safety video. Even a fall from a ladder can kill you, as can a tumble from the top deck of a party bus.

(There seems to be a recent resurgence in the number of people who believe the earth actually is flat, but that's probably got more to do with morons having finally figured out how to access the internet than any real increase in numbers.)

You can head in any direction at ground level, meaning North, South, East or West and keep going in a straight line before you end up back where you started 25,000 miles (40,000 km) later. The vertical axis is more difficult. Going down involves digging, so forget that, and going up requires flying machines. Or imagination. If it were possible to walk in the vertical direction, a power walker could finish her breakfast, walk up to the top of the O Zone, have a cup of tea and walk back home having worked up a big appetite for lunch. Not very far, in other words.

If you could drive a Tesla Roadster straight up, you could pour a cup of tea at home, drive up to the edge of the breathing zone, pull a hand-brake turn and when you got home your tea would have cooled just a little, enough to be at a perfect drinking temperature, without having to blow on it. The Tesla Roadster's the example used here because it is, so far, the only car to have actually travelled such a distance in the vertical axis. Unfortunately, the Roadster failed to turn around, so that cup of tea is now cold and bitter, like an oft-jilted lover.

You don't have to go all the way up to 12 kilometers to stop breathing. And why would anyone do that? Machu Picchu is only 2.4 km or 1.5 miles high and plenty of people find that's too high for comfort. In fact, any elevation above one mile can cause discomfort due to oxygen deprivation.

Something a planet designer might have perhaps considered is that if the 12km layer had been made 100km thick instead, there'd be more than enough good gases to keep everything in equilibrium and therefore no way stupid and inconsiderate humans could drive enough trucks to cause any climate change. But that's off topic.

As is the following brief digression.

Having sex in an aircraft, often in the unfeasibly cramped conditions of an economy class toilet, is generally, but erroneously, referred to as joining the mile-high club. The correct term should be the five-mile-high club, as that's the approximate cruising altitude of airliners at the time the phrase came into general use. The mile-high club, would be a lot more difficult to join as it would require getting down to business immediately after take off, while the aircraft is in a steep climb, thus increasing the gymnastic flexibility requirements for successful membership. It could also mean a delay in passengers getting their drinks and peanuts, because the seat belt lights would still be on and therefore the cabin crew would be the only ones likely to be getting busy. It is not known if the one-mile-high club has ever been joined during the descent phase of a flight, as most people who are keen to indulge in that sort of thing are unlikely to wait that long. The normal time for passengers to decide to sign in to the five-mile-high club is shortly after, or during, the third Bloody Mary.

It was the invention of the pressurized aircraft cabin that extended the O Zone for humans to five miles. Although experimentation in aircraft cabin pressurization began in the 1920s, the first pressurized airliner to enter widespread use was the Lockheed Constellation in 1943. Howard Hughes was rumored to have had a major hand in the design of the Constellation, and also to have been the founding member of the four-mile-high club (being roughly the cruising altitude of the Constellation) during early test flights, but Hughes himself denied the bit about his involvement in the design of the aircraft.

Machu Picchu and Everest aren't the only places on earth that are too high for comfort. There are lots of places more than a mile above sea level. A large part of Switzerland for instance. And Austria. In fact, there are sixteen countries whose average altitude is over 1.5km. These include Burundi, Rwanda, China, Afghanistan, Kyrgyzstan, Tajikistan, Nepal and Bhutan. That's a really big chunk of terrain that's short of oxygen, and therefore not comfortably habitable.

A lack of atmosphere is not only unromantic, it's also genuinely, physically cold, as there aren't enough molecules bashing around to maintain any sort of heat in the air. At a recent Formula One Grand Prix in Austria, it was a bright sunny day with a track surface temperature of 45°C (113°F) but an air temperature of only 18°C (64°F). You could slow fry an egg on the tarmac, while a frozen daiquiri would stay cool long enough in the shade to give you three ice cream headaches. Who'd want to live in such a place? Especially as the wearing of lederhosen and braces is mandatory, so you not only have to suffer the cold but also the indignity of looking like a village idiot.

The dry land bits of planet earth comprise about 29 percent of the surface area. The rest is mostly ocean. Coincidentally 29 percent of that 29 percent is a kilometer or more above sea level. Which means that approximately 80% of the surface area of a planet supposedly designed for human habitation is unsuitable even for human survival, let alone comfort. Spend too much time outside the habitable 20%, and you'll soon expire on account of having not enough air in your lungs, or too much water in your lungs.

Planet earth may look like a fairly sizeable object when observed from the moon, but just one fifth of its surface, just a coat of paint thick, is the total volume in which homo sapiens can possibly exist in the known universe.

In that way it's much like a BMW 6 series. Something fairly large overall but with a surprisingly tiny amount of usable space for the occupants. Not the ultimate passenger machine.

Total volume of the O zone - 816,000,000km^3 or 197,000,000 cubic miles.

Inhabitable volume of the O zone - 20% of the above. (You do the math.)

The O Zone - 9/10 (Fresh air is good.)

THE BLUE ZONES

The watery bits. The blue areas on the map make up the biggest zone by far. 71 percent of the surface of planet earth is ocean. Quite useful to mankind, but not as a place to live.

As far as mankind is concerned, oceans are a useful source of food. A big wet farm. Unlike most farms, oceans are difficult to establish ownership of, especially the South China Sea, and even more difficult to fence. The edges are nice in some places. Soft and sandy and useful for lying about on while you change your skin color and indulge in associated watersports. It can be fun to sail on. And that's about it. Oceans sure as hell cut down the surface area of planet earth as available living space for humans.

Unless you have a boat that's big enough to live on in which case you get to brag about having the biggest back yard in the world. Kanye West has been known to make a similar boast, but he wasn't talking about big boats.

Water is generally a very good thing. An absolute necessity for life. But if a human tries to survive by drinking the water

NOT VERY INTELLIGENT DESIGN TOO

from the ocean, he will die. If another human waters her garden and lawn with salty water, her garden and lawn will die. Although fresh water is absolutely essential to life on earth as we know it, 97% of the water on planet earth is salty. If this planet was designed for us, why are the oceans salty? Water that's not in oceans can also be useless on account of being frozen, or contaminated, both naturally and by human pollution, or by being inaccessible. In fact, less than one percent of planet earth's water is readily available to humans (and other thirsty creatures) in a form that sustains life. Arguably that's a fairly perverse design feature.

Lakes and rivers can sustain flourishing ecosystems without salt and if salmon can survive and thrive in both salt and fresh water why can't other forms of submarine food also do without salt? If salt free oceans resulted in us needing to add salt to smoke a salmon, that's a small inconvenience for an overabundance of fresh, delicious, life-sustaining water. People who add salt to their fish and chips might have to add a little more. Or eat a little less salt. Which is the healthy thing to do according to prevailing medical theory.

How would it be if the oceans were sugary instead of salty? Obese picnic goers could waddle down to the water's edge and refill their big gulp cups as often as they wished. Or they could swim and drink at the same time. In times gone by, children were warned not to swim too soon after lunch or they'd get cramp and drown. With sweet water, they'd be warned not to stay in the water too long after lunch or they'd get diabetes and die. Or have to go home wrapped in a towel because their clothes had become too small.

Oceans have another benefit in that they provide useful buffer zones between groups of people. People tend to form into large groups and declare themselves as independent nations, which can be a good thing. Nations, if responsibly governed, bring benefits in terms of infrastructure and education and healthcare and all that sort of stuff.

One of the not so good things about independent nations is that they often get too big for their boots. At which time they decide they'd like to have some of the land that belongs to the next door nation. So they have a war. Wars are much harder to fight with water in between the opposing sides. River crossings can impede the progress of an advancing panzer division. A channel can be a big enough deal that crossing it en masse warrants adding a capitalized letter D to the word day, but an ocean is often enough to make you reassess the whole idea. Something the Japanese should have done in 1941.

The vast amount of ocean that surrounds New Zealand has so far inoculated the little nation from invasion. (That is if you don't count the first Europeans as invaders, as some Maori might, or the Maori, as some Moriori might, had they survived.) Even without any sort of seriously plausible defense system, New Zealand remains secure on the basis of salt water. Also worth considering is that there's not much worth plundering. That is, everything that's great about the place falls into the category of non-removable. Hardly anybody, including most of the permanent residents, regard it as being God-given or in any other way spiritual or holy, and if you did happen to conquer it, what the hell would you do with it? It would most likely turn into an administration headache of migraine proportions and the conquerors would pull out and go home within a month or two.

Humans aren't the only creatures that dwell on this planet. We're outnumbered by thousands of different fish species but nobody knows for sure by how much. Or for how long. Maybe not so long given how nice they taste. Without being able to fence them into paddocks, fish are impossible to count, on top of which they never stay still for long. Some of them deliberately taunt fish counters by swimming in a big cloud then at the same moment they all change direction, and swim away really fast. This often happens just before a fish counter gets his leg bitten off by a shark.

Fish, like people in Southern California, never comment on the weather. Unlike the atmosphere, which can vary from blizzard to blistering heat, oceans are much more consistent and therefore provide a far more benign living environment than does the atmosphere. Local ocean temperatures vary by only a few degrees. In the tropics the variation is often as little as between 27 and 29°C (80 and 84°F) all year round. Day and night.

Tropical fish live in such a perfect natural environment they always look like they're on their way to a party. Or they're at the party. The only things that fuck up a tropical fish party are bigger fish, sharks and humans. When we arrive with nets or spear guns or hooks it's like Mardi Gras being attacked by Pablo Escobar's sicarios. Or Nice being decimated by a Jihadi truck driver.

As long as no humans or sharks show up, the life of a fish must be idyllic.

Nice day today.

As always.

Think it'll rain?

No such thing.

Might get cold later.

No chance.

There's a storm forecast.

Not down here.

Mommy fish never have to nag their kids to put on something warmer or to take a jacket to school. They're never late for school, because they're always in the school, and they don't need to build houses to sleep in or rent a storage unit to keep their extra stuff in.

Fish never get caught out in the rain or struck by lightning. And they never have to wipe their bottoms. On the down side they do swim in their own pee and poo, but it doesn't seem to bother them. Not surprising really. The same could be said of us and public swimming pools. At least the pee part.

Why wouldn't the creator have made the atmosphere of planet earth as consistent and benign as the oceans? In considering such a hypothetical, normal rules don't apply. Meaning the laws of nature and science may also be changed by the creator.

Given that oceans are far more agreeably tailored for fish than the atmosphere is for humans, and also that there's so much more ocean than land on the planet, it could easily be argued that if this planet was intelligently designed, then it was done so primarily for fish rather than for humans. (The same might also be said for ants or bacteria.)

Lakes and rivers are useful to humans and more easily managed than oceans but they must still be deducted from potential human living space in order to get an accurate overall picture.

The Blue Zones - 4/10 (for the edges and the yummy food)

(10/10 if you're a fish)

THE BROWN ZONES

Pretty much the opposite of oceans, deserts are areas that are almost as hostile to human existence, but on account of having too little water rather than too much.

Deserts come in four flavors. Ice cream, which is a dessert rather than a desert, comes in 31 or more flavors. A dessert is not just a misspelling of the word desert it also means something entirely different and isn't always a pudding. When you get your just desserts, it rarely involves food, although if you're out for dinner and decide that you'll have just dessert, it means you have a very unhealthy diet, and possibly a drug problem too. If your farm is just desert, that means it's worthless, unless there's a big pool of oil underneath it. Which may turn you into a Beverly Hillbilly or a murderous prince with a penchant for having your critics chopped up with a bone-saw. But enough of that distasteful topic.

The four flavors of desert -

Subtropical deserts are the cliché version, sand dunes, hot and dry all year round. Example, the Sahara.

Cool coastal deserts, such as the Atacama in Chile and Peru, have warm summers but cool winters.

Cold winter deserts, such as the Taklamakan Desert and others in China, Kazakhstan and Mongolia, have long, dry summers and even longer dry winters.

Polar deserts are, unsurprisingly, really, really cold, all the time.

Deserts have so little water that nothing can live there. Until David Attenborough arrives and discovers thousands of things that actually do live there. Including humans.

Most human desert dwellers are nomads, who spend their lives moving from one deserted location to another in search of a better place to live, sometimes including better grazing for their livestock. The fact that they've been doing this for thousands of years without ever finding their way out of the desert makes it easy to surmise that their navigation skills are questionable.

It also makes TomTom's naming choice for their first off-road and wilderness GPS device, the Nomad, seem like one of the worst marketing decisions of all time. Albeit a slightly better choice than the Fukawi, which also reportedly, and bewilderingly, made the short list. (The Fukawi are the shortest of all Pygmy tribes, most famous for regularly getting lost in the tall grasslands of their habitat and their haka-style chant, "We're the Fukawi".) The Nomad was withdrawn from the market after an investigative reporter for National Geographic broke the story that at least 85% of Nomad users never made it home from their wilderness adventure. TomTom's defense, in the ensuing class action lawsuit, was that purchasers of the Nomad were knowingly buying into a new Nomadic lifestyle. Amazingly the jury agreed with them and so the families left behind were forced to start a series of crowd-funded search and rescue missions, which succeeded in finding only one of the more than twelve hundred missing adventurers.

Cliff Merryweather Trimball, 46, left his home in Michigan to hike the Appalachian Trail and was found three years later in the company of an Argentinian woman in a yurt in the Gobi Desert in Mongolia. Trimball's Nomad device was no longer functional due to a flat battery, although a reliable power source would reportedly have made no difference to the likelihood of Trimball returning home.

The Nomad wasn't the only marketing snafu made by TomTom. The introduction of the Turnaround, once again poorly named, after one of the most annoying pop songs of the early seventies, was an abject failure. The Tom Tom Turnaround had a serious firmware glitch that would keep reasserting itself even after repeated updates. The glitch involved correctly identifying one way roads, but incorrectly identifying the direction of the traffic flow. The Turnaround was at its worst after automatically updating to firmware version 6.9 when it started giving directions onto freeways against the flow for every search entered, even when the nearest freeway was many miles away from the most direct route.

TomTom's legal team successfully argued the class action lawsuit against the Turnaround, saying that if users followed the most important direction, which was prominently displayed on both the box, and at the top of the instruction sheet, namely "Turnaround", they would not have been involved in any fatal head-on collisions.

According to National Geographic more than one billion people live in desert regions. Hard to believe until you take into consideration another barely plausible and disappointing fact that only one tenth of the world's deserts are made up of sand dunes. Sand is not the criteria by which an inhospitable expanse is classified as a desert. The criteria is rainfall. Less than 25cm or 10 inches per year means desert. And they often get less than that. In fact, less than zero is not all that uncommon and occurs when evaporation prevails over precipitation.

As well as being dry and occasionally sandy, deserts are most often associated with being hot. The Sahara often reaches 50°C (122°F). But, in keeping with the disappointingly small proportion of sand dunes in deserts, not all of them are hot. Some are really cold. Like the one in Antarctica, which is always cold, obviously, and the Gobi which is not always cold, but can get down to fifteen below, on account of its elevation.

Deserts are present on every continent including Australia. Robert Bogucki was a fireman from Alaska who became deliberately lost in Australia's Great Sandy Desert. Bogucki had become a religious zealot who wanted to test his own faith with 40 days alone in the wilderness. His plan was thought to have developed the previous year, soon after he was called to extinguish a burning bush. He said that being rescued after 43 days was highly significant, because that was the same number of days that Jesus spent in the wilderness plus the three days that Jesus spent being sort of almost dead.

When it was pointed out to Bogucki that the cost to Australian taxpayers for his search and rescue was $72,000 he realized that was a thousand times the exact number (no need to pull an extra three out of his ass this time) of virgins that would await him in heaven, were he an extremist Muslim, so he bought a prayer mat and an AK47 and gave up shaving. His conversion to Islam will come in handy should he hear a calling one day to repay Australia for his rescue costs. Muslims don't believe in the concept of paying interest on loans, so he won't feel any compunction to pay for the cost of using other people's money that he so brazenly squandered.

Most earthlings regard deserts as places to avoid. But given that there are people who will voluntarily risk their lives to surf giant waves, hold their breath while diving to testicle-crushing depths, climb mountains already littered with discarded trash and frozen corpses, and walk on tight ropes across ravines all in the name of sport, it's not really surprising to find humans who can look out across miles of inhospitable, barren wasteland and see a race course.

The 4 Deserts Race Series is, unsurprisingly, a series of races that involves four deserts. The Atacama, the Gobi, the Sahara and the one in Antarctica, which doesn't seem to have a name, as the whole continent is pretty much one big desert. Each race is 155 miles (250km), split up over seven days, which makes it seem not so bad until you realize that you're not allowed to use cars, tractors, motorbikes, camels or huskies to help you on your way. Not only do you have to complete the distance on foot, you have to carry all your stuff with you, including food. And people actually pay to do this. Thousands of them. Lunatics.

The Atacama Desert also features as part of the Dakar rally, in which you may use motorized vehicles, including huge trucks which look totally ridiculous plowing their way over massive sand dunes, sometimes crushing wayward spectators as they go. The Dakar rally used to take place between Paris and Dakar, across parts of North Africa, but was shifted to South America to cut down on the number of competitors and spectators being shot by bandits of the Sahara.

The deserts of North Africa are also famous for other types of shooting, including wars and the movie Lawrence of Arabia. At one time Germany and Britain thought it was a good idea to settle their differences by fighting huge tank battles in a desert. The German panzer divisions were led by the Desert Fox, aka Generalfeldmarschall Johannes Erwin Eugen Rommel, whose last recorded tipple was cyanide. But that was a few years later. Rommel's panzer divisions were routed by the Desert Rats, led by Field Marshal Bernard Law Montgomery, 1st Viscount Montgomery of Alamein, KG, GCB, DSO, PC, DL. As well as winning the crucial final battle, Monty also easily won the longest name and title competition.

Deserts make up about a third of the land area on earth. Leaving just two thirds available for human habitation. When we subtracted the oceans and the places without enough oxygen, we were left with just twenty percent of the earth's surface as potential human habitat. Two thirds of twenty percent, is 13.3 percent. Salt loving fish get 71 percent.

If planet earth was designed for human habitation, why make so much of it impossible for humans to live on?

Deserts - 1/10 (some humans find amusement in them)

THE WHITE ZONES

The White Zones have just a few things in common with the Blue and Brown Zones, the main one being a shortage of nice places to set up camp and raise a family.

As can be deduced from the name, the White Zones are the places covered in snow and ice most, if not all, of the time. They include the polar regions - the places where the sun don't shine in winter, and the mountainous regions - which can be fun on a sunny day. As long as there are chairlifts. Despite their similar level of hostility to human survival, the terrain of the White Zones couldn't be more varied. The mountainous regions are mountainous. The Antarctic is mountainous in parts, and actually has the highest average elevation of all continents, but it also has lots of lower bits and it would still be cold and miserable even if it were flat. Most of the Arctic, including the North Pole itself and a continent-sized area around it, is neither mountainous nor lowlands on account of being frozen water rather than dirt and rocks.

There are less trees in the White Zones than there are humans. In fact, there are none. Just as mountains have a tree line, so do the polar circles. The tree line of the North Polar Circle may sound like part of a subway system but by the time it's warm enough to warrant a mass transit project in any polar area, the rest of the planet will have fried to a crisp. The northern tree line is partially imaginary as it encompasses mostly iced water, even though it also crosses Norway, Sweden, Finland, Russia, Alaska, Canada, Greenland and Iceland.

If earth were a man's head, the North Pole would resemble the lid of Friar Tuck, with a bare dome, surrounded by foliage. Most depictions of Tuck show a very clean line, uniformly dividing shiny pate from luxuriant growth, but because the northern tree line crosses so many islands and land masses, the edge of the pate would be ragged and patchy.

The southern tree line is totally imaginary, in that it would fall entirely along an unbroken line of ocean. Think Vin Diesel or Dwayne the Rock Johnson doing a headstand.

The fact that trees can't survive in the White Zones should be all the evidence required to deter mankind from ever bothering to go there. However, humans are not only the smartest creatures on the planet, we're also the stupidest. Someone started a lie about lemmings flocking off cliffs and thereby committing mass suicide on a scale that would embarrass Jim Jones, but it turned out to be bullshit, possibly in an attempt to find an animal dumber than humans and make us all feel better about ourselves.

Jim Jones has nothing to be proud of as he convinced just under a thousand people to kill themselves and their children, whereas other cults have started wars of conquest that have resulted in the deaths of millions, and an ongoing wretched existence for billions. But that's beyond the scope of the subject at hand.

The urge to climb mountains is one example of human stupidity. It's abundantly obvious from the base of any mountain without a chairlift, that nothing good will be found up there. No peach trees. No beach parties. No hamburger stands. No cocktail bars. Nothing. It will become increasingly cold, uncomfortable and dangerous the further up you go. Why bother?

Expeditions to explore the polar regions may be excused however, or even possibly celebrated, as they were genuine journeys into the unknown with important discoveries being a real, albeit unlikely, possibility. Although less sphincter-puckeringly scary, polar expeditions were, in days gone by, just as dangerous as mountain climbing expeditions. A cursory look at the equipment available back then shows that there were, and probably still are, a number of people who don't instinctively recoil at the thought of losing their fingers and toes.

Pytheas, a contemporary of Aristotle and Alexander the Great, is believed by some to have been the first explorer to reach the Arctic Circle. In 325 BC, he sailed from Marseilles, past Gibraltar to Brittany, then Cornwall and on further northward, perhaps to the Shetland Islands, perhaps even further north, then possibly circumnavigating Britain before returning, having failed to find the source of tin that he had been seeking.

Pytheas was clearly an idiot. Firstly, a wiser man would have asked the merchants already bringing tin to Marseilles where it came from, rather than getting in a boat to go and look for it. Secondly, having set out from the rather idyllic setting of the Mediterranean, Pytheas sailed a course that took him to increasingly less pleasant locales. A wise man would have turned back well before reaching Brittany, a man of average intelligence certainly at Cornwall, a fool at any other landfall on the way to Scotland, but only a complete moron would have completed the journey of Pytheas.

The reportage of Pytheas was widely regarded as fantasy, so just why his name has survived in the historical record is a mystery.

Some Vikings, including Gardar Svavarssonsonsson and Bjorn Ulfssonsonsson, are thought to have ventured as far as the ice shelf of the Arctic, both as a result of navigational errors. But, like Pytheas and any number of unlucky fishermen, anyone can exaggerate or straight out make shit up. If they'd had their wits about them Gardar and Bjornsson would have headed south, to the Med.

Rather than tin, or whatever it was the Vikings were looking for, the Holy Grail of the Arctic Circle was the Northwest Passage. Like the Holy Grail, many people set out to search for the Northwest Passage although there was no evidence that it actually existed. This didn't deter the explorers however, as they share common DNA with mountain climbers, so pointless, dangerous missions naturally appeal to them. A Northwest Passage, should it exist, would potentially become a very lucrative trade route, although just how this would benefit its discoverers is a mystery. It's not as if they could claim it in the name of their nation, or even charge a toll for its use.

For logistical reasons alone the setting up of toll booths would be problematic. A spell of poor weather, not uncommon in the Arctic, would be enough to almost guarantee that resupply missions would be greeted by a succession of toll collectors frozen stiff in their poorly insulated toll huts.

Attempts to find the Northwest Passage were not only foolhardy but unbelievably numerous. If you scroll down the Wikipedia page entitled List of Arctic Expeditions, you're more likely to suffer from RSI than make it to the end.

In 1539 an attempt was made to find the Northwest Passage by sailing up the east coast of the Baja California Peninsula. The theory was that there may be a channel connecting the Pacific with the Gulf of Saint Lawrence. You have to admire their optimism, setting off on a great journey of exploration with nothing more than a hunch to go on. At least in this instance, they weren't in danger of losing any expedition members or body parts to frostbite.

The first traversal of the Northwest Passage via dog sled was accomplished by Greenlander, Knud Rasmussensensen, who took sixteen months to travel from the Atlantic to the Pacific from 1922 to 1924. This is a confusing record. As the raison d'être of the Northwest Passage was to be a maritime trade route, traversing it in anything other than a boat shouldn't really count. It's like going to Kitty Hawk and traversing the course flown by the Wright Flyer on a bicycle. Would that be anything? Not really. Nothing more than a ride on a bicycle. If you had a grizzly bear on the back of your bike it might be something. But, nah.

All the death and suffering involved in trying to discover the Northwest Passage didn't result in making it any more than an extended exercise in futility. If everyone had stayed home and sat around a nice warm fire, they would have found it just as quickly. Because that's exactly what happened.

Partly as a result of mankind's huge appetite for keeping warm as well as keeping on the move, we've burnt enough fossil fuels to open up the Northwest Passage like a clam in boiling water. If the polar ice cap continues to melt at the current rate, then the next record set will likely be by Bjorn Fredrikksonsenson barefoot waterskiing the passage behind a foiling catamaran.

Even if we succeed in melting all the ice up there, the Arctic will still not be a suitable place for human habitation. It will have merely changed its reason for being inhospitable, from a White Zone to a Blue Zone.

People often erroneously state that when the Arctic ice cap melts, half the cities on earth will end up under water. This is not true as anyone can prove by doing a simple experiment with ice and a glass of water. Fill the glass with ice, then top it off with water so that you have mini icebergs sticking out the top. Wait for the ice to melt. How much water spills over the top? None. Water expands when frozen, and ice shrinks when it melts. The spare space created by the melted ice is taken up by the 10% of iceberg that was above the water.

Thus the melting of the Arctic ice cap will have almost zero effect on ocean levels.

The same is not true on the opposite side of the globe. Down there most of the ice isn't floating. It's sitting on top of a great big land mass. When it melts it'll all run down to the sea, and that will be a problem. Unless we grow gills and relearn the joys of living a life aquatic.

The ice that covers Antarctica is really, really thick. On average the ice is 2.16 km (1.34 miles) deep across the whole thing. It contains more than 60% of the fresh water in and on the whole planet. If that lot melted completely, it would raise sea levels by 58 meters (190 feet). That's roughly the height of a ten story building.

The result would be more available space for humans to live on the Antarctic continent, but less space on all the other continents. Plus it would be hard to get to Antarctica because all the ports and marinas that we currently use to set sail would be a long way under water. And it'd still be really cold and unpleasant down there.

The amount of loss of habitable space on the planet overall, as a result of such melting, would require some research and a lot of calculation to accurately establish. Someone's probably already done that.

The Antarctic is just as cold and dangerous as the Arctic and therefore just as enticing to explorers. There are reports of expeditions dating back almost to the dawn of handwriting, but many of these were, like the Arctic versions, crazy people heading off to extremely cold climates only to return with a shortage of digits and crew members, or not to return at all. After hundreds of ventures, it was finally in about 1850 that the first documented landing occurred on mainland Antarctica.

Following the confirmation that such a place actually existed, frostbite fans began to jostle for position to be first to reach the South Pole. When one considers that this race began, informally, some hundreds of years earlier, the finish was remarkably close. Ronald Amundsensensson's expedition got there on the 14th of December 1911, followed by Robert

Falcon Scott's expedition just over a month later on the 17th of January 1912.

Amundsen afterwards commented on the sanity of cold climate adventurers: "Never has a man achieved a goal so diametrically opposed to his wishes. The area around the North Pole—devil take it—had fascinated me since childhood, and now here I was at the South Pole. Could anything be more crazy?"

Reaching the South Pole is very much like reaching the top of a mountain. You have to turn around and head for home quick smart, because if you hang around you'll die.

Amundsensson dallied just long enough to pitch a tent, erect a pole, hang two flags on it and leave the explorer's equivalent of a thumbed nose for Scott's team, in the form of a letter addressed to King Haakon, his king, not Scott's, and a request for Scott to deliver it. How those pesky Norwegians must have laughed and laughed all the way home thinking about Scott's face when he saw the letter.

We'll never know Scott's exact reaction to the letter because, unlike Amundsonssen, Scott and his brave lads did dally too long out in the cold. Some time later, bodies and artifacts from Scott's expedition were discovered, including note books, in which Scott, like Amundssensensonsen, acknowledged the foolhardiness of his endeavors.

"The Pole. Yes, but under very different circumstances from those expected... Great God! This is an awful place and terrible enough for us to have labored to it without the reward of priority. Well, it is something to have got here." This was, of course, written before he realized he was not going to make it back, which may have made his description of the place even less favorable.

Amundsenssen made it back without losing so much as a single finger or toe, let alone a life. That is, if you don't count the dogs, who were regarded initially as man's best friend, then as sled pullers, and finally as food, as the expedition proceeded. On the way back, the dogs seemed to sense that if they ran faster, and therefore got home sooner, more of them would make the cut. Or avoid the cut. Thus they arrived home in just 99 days, 10 less than scheduled.

Of the 52 good boys that set out on the journey, just 11 survived, 6 more than scheduled. It is not known for certain there is such a thing as canine PTSD, but it's hard to imagine anything much more traumatizing for a dog than enduring the extreme hardship of a long polar journey, then being forced into cannibalism whilst watching your friends being chopped up and eaten by the men you previously trusted.

One of Amundsensonssen's expedition team, Hjalmar Johansensonsen, died of a self-inflicted gunshot wound on the 9th of January 1913. It is not known whether he was a cat person or a dog person.

The aftermath of the Scott expedition was an icy shitstorm of recrimination and finger pointing that went on for decades, and may still not be over, but in one of his final written notes Scott himself documented that "our wreck is certainly due to this sudden advent of severe weather, -30°F (-34°C) in the day, -47°F (-44°C) at night". Severely cold weather in the Antarctic? Who could've predicted that?

About forty countries operate research stations in the Antarctic and there's even a smidgen of tourist activity. Most of the research stations are seasonal, with about 4,000 people there during the summer months and about 1,000 in winter. These numbers, as a percentage of world population, are approximately exactly equal to zero, demonstrating that human life is not realistically sustainable down there. And neither are marriages.

It's a well known, but impossible to verify, fact that almost everybody who spends any time at an Antarctic research station indulges in some form of marriage-threatening infidelity. It may be the cold, or possibly the cold, that encourages scientists and their guests to jump under warm furry covers and screw like bunnies. Huskies look almost as cute as bunnies provided you don't think about the fact that their Antarctic history involves most of them eating each other.

Tourists visit the continent mostly by cruise ship, and most are happy to spectate from the deck, rather than board a Zodiac for a journey to land. Clambering down rope netting to board a rubber ducky from the vertical flanks of a cruise ship is not recommended for drunk, overweight geriatrics, so that rules out most passengers.

Large commercial passenger jets have flown sightseeing tourists over Antarctica at various times since the 1970s. Why anybody would voluntarily get on a plane for a long flight that'll theoretically end up back at exactly the same place is a mystery.

Despite the nomenclature, the Antarctic is the only continent on earth where there are no ants.

Mountains are pretty things to look at. And fun to ski down. But they are very dangerous to walk up. If you want a closer look, a helicopter's not a bad option, provided you don't want to look at really tall mountains, because helicopters require a certain amount of air to fly safely and there's not so much of it when you get right up there. But chairlifts and helicopters aren't the only option.

On the north face of the Eiger there's a window. The window is on the platform of a railway station called Eigerwand, which translates as Wall of Eiger. It would probably be the only railway station on earth at which everybody who got off the train also got back on the very same train, before it left the station, if it weren't for another station on the same line on the south side of the mountain called Eismeer, where the same thing happens. There's no way for passengers to access these stations apart from by train on the single railway line, although there is an exit door of sorts at the Eigerwand station which opens directly onto to the Eiger's north face. It should not need pointing out that it serves no practical purpose as far as train travelers are concerned.

The sole purpose of the Eigerwand station is its famous window, which was designed to provide tourists with a dollop of alpine eye candy and, for those present at exactly the right moment, some live action in the form of mountain climbers falling to their deaths.

The door was almost useful in 1936, when a group of climbers abseiled down past the Eigerwand station following a failed attempt to scale the peak. A railway guard opened the door and suggested the climbers may wish to return to safety in the comfort of a railway carriage. But he needn't have bothered. He was talking to mountain climbers. They said they were fine and were shortly thereafter smashed by an avalanche.

Andreas Hinterstoisser was unclipped from the group at the moment the avalanche hit. His pulverized, frozen remains were located at the bottom of the mountain some days later. Willy Angerer also died immediately as he was smashed into the face of the mountain, fortunately not breaking any windows in the process. Edi Rainer quickly joined his comrades in death as the "safety rope" around his waist, now heavily weighed down by the dead and dying, asphyxiated him. Toni Kurz dangled from the rope with his dead friends for three days as more mountain climbers risked their lives to come to his rescue.

The rescue was one of the most rapidly responded to climbing emergencies in history, mostly because of the convenience of the railway station, which the rescuers were not too proud to use. They got close enough to reach out and touch Kurz, but Kurz could not reach back to save himself as his whole arm was frozen, and he was exhausted from lack of sleep. A frozen shoulder can make sleeping very difficult, so a fully frozen arm and hand would certainly have put the kibosh on any hope of a good night's kip. Despite being so close to rescue, Kurz was too far gone, and he slipped into the heart of darkness as his despairing, would-be rescuers looked on.

The Eigerwand Station was closed in 2016, which diminished the opportunity for passengers to view falling climbers. But not completely. Trains still pass through the station. They just don't stop. So the odds of spotting a tumbler from the window of a moving train are not good.

Randall Higenbotham, 64, of Scunthorpe, had not heard about the closure of the Eigerwand Station when he headed to Switzerland for his three-week alpine holiday in 2017. Randall had saved hard for seven years to fulfil his dream of experiencing a climbing season first hand. On his arrival in Grindelwald, he heard about the closure of the Eigerwand Station. Initially crestfallen, he did some research and soon formulated a plan. He disembarked at Stollenloch, a station used by climbers not far from Eigerwand, and then walked up through the tunnel to Eigerwand Station.

Randall went straight to the window and set up camp there, not moving for three days. At the end of the third day, having filled all his empty bottles and absolutely gagging for a dump, Randall walked back down the line to the next station, caught the last train and returned to his single room, shared bathroom, accommodation in a modest pension in the village of Grindelwald. He had by this time also realized that there was no point in spending nights up at the window, because climbers tuck themselves into hammocks and rarely fall after dark. Also, because of the dark, Randall wouldn't see a passing climber if he or she did fall.

For the next seventeen days Randall rose at dawn, caught the first train, got off at Stollenloch, and walked up through the tunnel to spend the daylight hours at the viewing window, returning to Grindelwald each evening.

On his last day, Randall arose as usual and headed up to the Eigerwand window. His diary had only one entry. On the fourth day he had seen a group of three climbers, roped together, making good progress up the face. They were some distance from him so he couldn't tell much about them. They climbed out of sight in less than an hour. Apart from that, nothing.

For the occasion of his last day in the alps, Randall, not normally a drinker, took a bottle of apfelschnapps up the mountain. He felt it was appropriate to toast the great north face as he had a premonition, as well as a shortage of funds, that indicated it was quite possibly the last time he'd ever see it.

The sun began to set. Randall's holiday adventure was nearly done. He turned from the window and started to climb down onto the railway track. At that moment he heard a scream from behind him. Randall spun around on the spot, catching a fleeting glimpse of a blur going past the window. Randall's face lit up in glee, but only for the briefest instant as his foot slipped on the wet rail.

Randall had, some days earlier, given up on peeing in bottles, realizing that he could hear an approaching train in plenty of time to avoid being caught urinating onto the track in the glare of the headlight.

The sudden rotation of his head gave Randall no chance of controlling the momentum of his massively fat belly as his foot slipped on the slick, narrow surface of the rail, and he crashed down hard, smashing his head on the rocky ground while simultaneously twisting his ankle and fracturing his wrist and shoulder blade.

He spent almost an hour slipping in and out of consciousness, in part due to concussion and in part due to excruciating pain which was only minimally alleviated by the liter of schnapps he'd consumed over the previous four hours. Randall's ankle was trapped under the rail, and the combination of his more than ample weight, his arm injury, and the pain associated with even the slightest movement, prevented him from moving at all.

The train driver, who had, coincidentally, also been consuming schnapps for the previous four hours, hesitated in disbelief before slamming on the brakes. But it was too late and Randall Higenbotham became the 65th person to die as a result of a fall on the Eiger since the infamous 1936 tragedy that inspired his alpine holiday.

Of all the tales told of the human experience in the White Zones, only three of them have happy endings. Which is really all one needs to know when considering the White Zones.

Whilst inhospitable to humans, the White Zones do provide homes for a number of animal species, both land and water based. The Arctic has polar bears, the Antarctic has penguins and the mountains have goats. There's no clear cut answer as to how or why one married couple of each of the above were persuaded to make their long journeys to Noah's Boat Yard and get aboard his ark. There's also no clear explanation as to how the polar bears survived for 150 days without eating at least one or both seals, or tasting penguin for the first time.

A pair of foxes could easily account for a few dozen chickens during such a cruise. It's not widely reported in such a way but it seems logical that a steerage ticket on Noah's Ark was the same thing as a place on a shelf in the pantry.

Given that a simple 99 day Antarctic mission ended up as a dog eat dog struggle for survival, and that the primary diet of so many animals is other animals, it's amazing that Noah's Ark didn't turn into a huge hunger games cage fight for scarce meat resources. It doesn't require much thinking time to conclude that the explanation can only be found in miracles and mysterious ways, which exist in a different universe from reality and common sense.

Unsurprisingly, the mountain with the biggest reputation is the biggest mountain. Everest. The name should be a warning to climbers that there's a good chance they will indeed rest there forever, but that doesn't deter them. Each year more than a thousand people decide to give it a go, clambering up past the more than 200 ever-resting dead bodies that line the route.

On average each climber spends about two months in the vicinity of Everest and will produce about 30Kg or 60 pounds of poo. "The peak has become a fecal time bomb, and the mess is gradually sliding back toward base camp," according to Grayson Schaffer of Outside magazine.

The Arctic and Antarctic circles each cover about 4% of Earth's surface, while mountains account for about 20% of the land area.

The White Zones - 1/10 (uninhabitable eye candy)

THE RED ZONES

The Red Zones are the places where people shouldn't spend much time, let alone live, on account of the area being either on fire, about to be on fire, erupting and spurting molten rock, or shaking too much.

Volcanoes should really be tough enough not to need to hang around in gangs, but most of them do. Even when one appears to be a lone pimple on a wide expanse of flat ground, it can be thought of as being a bit like an iceberg, showing just the tip, even though there's an ocean of hot, boiling pus running in rivers beneath the surface, often stretching for thousands of miles.

Ring of Fire may refer to a Johnny Cash song, a post-vindaloo sphincter condition, or the volcanic area that runs all the way around the edge of the Pacific Ocean, one of the aforementioned underground lava rivers.

Volcanic fields can be like violent, alcoholic husbands who've been on the wagon for years. Just because they haven't erupted recently doesn't mean you're safe. Sometimes the recurrence of the old behavior comes with early warning signs, perhaps the loss of a job or a workplace humiliation, a few small tremors, perhaps a minor earthquake or a few puffs of smoke. And just like an abused wife who remains both in hope and denial, millions of people still build houses along the fault lines of the Ring of Fire.

Auckland, New Zealand, spreads itself over a field of about 48 volcanoes. Stand atop any of the seven big ones and you can look around and easily see the others close by. The largest and most recently formed is Rangitoto Island, which rises magnificently out of Auckland harbor and appears as the symbol in most logos representing the region. It last erupted about 600 years ago. Auckland's volcanoes are dormant, which may give people a false sense of security but dormant means asleep, not dead. The field is not extinct, so new eruptions may occur at any time. And given that the centre of the city is built pretty much directly atop the centre of the field, any decent sized eruption would have a catastrophic effect.

Aucklanders aren't the only people apparently stupid enough to live on top of a danger zone. Other parts of the Ring of Fire include the San Andreas Fault, which isn't so big on spurting lava, rather it reminds residents of California of its presence by randomly, and without warning, cracking open and swallowing them.

Volcanologists and seismologists are second only to economists in terms of lack of accuracy in predicting future events in their field of expertise. In order of honesty, it goes volcanologists, seismologists and other scientists, who openly admit that they don't know what they don't know, then a dead heat between fortune tellers (none of whom has ever won a major lottery or been paid out on a Kentucky Derby winner) and economists and financial commentators, who pretend that what they do is scientific, yet whose advice in financial columns is as bankable as a used bus ticket.

"Wow, I didn't see that coming", is something volcanologists say fairly often but is rarely uttered by economists with one very famous exception. Alan Greenspan admitted that he was "in a state of shocked disbelief" following the financial meltdown of 2008 when he testified before the House Committee on Oversight and Government Reform. He also admitted that his ideology pushed him to make mistakes, that he had since found a flaw in it, and his belief had been shaken. All of which sounds more like theology than science and somewhat akin to Stephen Hawking admitting to being shocked to find that his faith in astrology had been shaken.

And yet many politicians and others choose to have faith in economists rather than believe what scientists say when it comes to climate change. But enough of that digression.

A dormant field such as the one beneath Auckland can produce a new volcanic event any time, perhaps tomorrow, but on average, some time between a few hundred and a few thousand years. Although volcanic fields pose an ongoing danger, they do not affect the quality of life available on top of them as long as residents are content to forget about it. In fact, volcanic soil is very good for growing produce, so there is a reward for the risk. Especially for vegetarians.

When close by and unheralded, an erupting volcano must be absolutely terrifying. Many people have experienced a mild earthquake. Or two, or three. They often arrive in groups. Even the mildest grade of earthquake, one that results in no damage at all, can be quite an unsettling sensation.

It may have to do with the concept that the ground we rely on is suddenly not reliable. People who live in quake prone areas do get used to it, just as air travelers get used to turbulence, but when a larger than normal quake hits it's as unnerving as seeing flames and fan parts exiting the starboard engine over the middle of the Pacific Ocean.

An excavator digging foundations next door can shake your house as much as a mild quake, but because you understand the source of the vibrations, the reaction doesn't involve existential fear, merely annoyance and how much more fuckin' dirt do those useless fuckin' bastards have to fuckin' well dig? What the fuck are they doing over there, looking for a middle earth trade route to fuckin' China?

Solid ground, down to earth, grounded, a firm footing and a solid foundation are all expressions that reference our connection to, and faith in, planet earth. It's home. Safe. Where we belong. The concept of home is so strong in most of us that getting back there often serves the purpose of a happy ending in an uplifting novel or movie. When our home unexpectedly moves beneath our feet, we feel displaced. Instant refugees with absolutely nothing to rely on. The refugee analogy doesn't hold for long because for most of us, when the ground stops shaking everything's okay again.

For some people when the earth stops shaking, life can even take a turn for the better. George Right was a struggling artist who had been painting straight lines of color with meticulous accuracy for many years. Becoming increasingly frustrated by the amount of time required to paint each work, Right invented a system for painting many colored stripes simultaneously using a long straight edge which he dragged across his canvas. His first efforts were a failure, with smudging and blurring of the lines, and a disappointing lack of precision. Nevertheless, he persisted. One day his studio was shaken by a quake that measured 4.5 on the Richter Scale. The resulting masterpiece was an explosion of muddled and jagged fault lines that resembled the output of a seismograph on LSD and was the first of a series of paintings that shook the art world, and propelled the artist to international fame and fortune.

George Right had for some time been worrying that his pedestrian sounding name was one of the things holding his career back. He changed his name to Gerhard Richter as a tip of the hat to the creator of the scale on which a 4.5 had been responsible for changing one of his signature styles. Whether it was the name change or the new form of painting that brought about his acceptance by the cognoscenti will probably never be known.

Volcanologists are like storm chasers, mountaineers and old time arctic explorers. They identify something life threatening and then see how close they can get to it without accidentally committing suicide. Given the large numbers of such thrill seekers it's surely only a matter of time before there's a TV game show version of Russian Roulette. One more spin and the cost of a lavish funeral is guaranteed, three more spins and you win a million dollars.

While the threat of death by fire or mass burial in Red Zones doesn't stop people living in locations that present otherwise good conditions, they do beg the question that if planet earth was designed as the perfect place for humans to live, why make some places look and feel almost perfect, and then deliberately place a mine field underneath them?

As a naturally occurring feature of nature, we are beginning to understand what goes on beneath the planet's surface from a scientific perspective. But what sort of creator would deliberately design, build and then conceal, gigantic randomly exploding land mines beneath the feet of people who had no idea about the potential death and destruction that might strike them, without warning, at any moment.

According to the Bible (Psalms 104:32), "He looketh on the earth, and it trembleth: he toucheth the hills, and they smoke." Thereby adding capriciousness to a thoroughly evil design.

Red Zones present a clear threat to human existence even if that threat is not constant. Winter is often thought of as the least pleasant of seasons, unless you live somewhere that has a fire season. People who live in fire season Red Zones need to be ready to jump in their trucks and abandon their homes and life possessions at a moment's notice. If they let their cell phone battery die, or they forget to turn on their transistor radio, there's a good chance they'll be incinerated along with their truck and everything else they own.

But there are a few good things that can be said about wildfires. They're not racist or elitist. Wildfires pick on poor Greek citizens and rich Californian wine makers alike. Many Australian trees don't mind an occasional blaze that clears the scrub around their trunks, being the Ozzie bush version of natural manscaping.

Wildfires are a bit like volcanoes and earthquakes in that they occur in predictable locations. They're not quite as capriciously evil in that you can see them coming. But apart from that they're mostly on the evil side of the ledger.

The Red Zones - 1/10

THE BLACK ZONES

The Black Zones include caves, challenging ski runs, areas around oil rigs, and the deepest points of the oceans. The deepest points of the oceans occupy a lot more surface area than caves and ski runs, but are already covered by, the Blue Zones.

Caves are some of the places where the sun don't shine and make up such a small percentage of the planet they're hardly worth a mention. They're also often underneath land that is habitable, so, in that sense they're not significant. But as a thing in the human psyche, they do occupy space. Caves feature in religious myths, legends, and folklore from all times and places, and therefore have a place in the story of humanity, so they need to be acknowledged.

In practical terms, they often have suitable walls for painting the outlines of hands on. They're a good place for storing wine and for drinking wine, and they're often handy, when in a hidden cove, for storing pirate treasure including silver and golden goblets. They're also perfect for storing temporarily deceased prophets (whose blood may at some future time turn into wine), and... that's about it.

Although, way back when humanity was even stupider than we are today, people lived in them. The plus side was that caves kept the rain off your head. But they're damp and cold and even with the romantic glow of a campfire to marginally alleviate the damp and cold, fires posed a serious risk of asphyxiation as there was usually no way for the smoke to escape. The main form of smoke recycling was through the lungs of the cave dwellers. Perhaps this is how we learned to smoke.

Cave men used to go out hunting for blond women. If they found one they would hit her on the head with a massive club, grab her by the ponytail, and drag her back to their cave for procreation purposes. People over the age of 50 learned about this in school with the aid of story books illustrated with cartoons. It was portrayed in a way that clearly indicated the authors, and contemporary adults, thought the whole thing was very amusing.

Much like the old illustrated children's books about Arab harems with sex slaves guarded by eunuchs. They were never called sex slaves of course, they were the Sultan's wives and concubines who lived a luxurious life of milk-bathed leisure, and if they were routinely and repeatedly raped for their whole useful lives at the hands of the men who owned them, it was never mentioned in the beautifully illustrated books.

The most horrifying thought is that in many circles in many countries, women continue to be treated in much the same way. But enough of that disgusting depravity.

Back to the cave men.

There was no hint that the mating rituals of cavemen were what we would now call assault with grievous bodily harm followed by violent rape, and that cave women were essentially sex slaves who were in danger of death or serious brain damage every time they were captured for the mating procedure. The cranial danger was because the clubs utilized by cave men for seduction purposes were generally illustrated to be the size and shape of about a dozen baseball bats strapped together.

Fred Flintstone and Barney Rubble were atypical cavemen in this regard. Wilma and Betty would never have put up with any such nonsense from them.

Caves are more suited to bears than humans. If a human enters a cave, there is always the danger that a bear is already in there. If you wake a bear, chances are it'll be in the mood for breakfast, and if you're the slowest runner of the available humans, then you're it.

Entering a cave with no bears inside isn't much safer. The bear may have just popped out to take a shit in the woods, and if you're in her cave when she returns, it's not really going to matter how fast you can run. If there are lots of you, such as a faith-based youth group, you may be able to hide at the back and sneak out with any other survivors when momma bear takes a post-lunch nap.

After caves, people built little huts out of rocks, and eventually great big stone castles which were almost as cold and damp as caves on account of their vast size, the building materials, lack of insulation and weather sealing, and the amount of firewood required to heat them.

Caves are where crazy people go to do an idiotic thing called spelunking. The name of the hobby pretty much sums up what sort of person gets a thrill out of something most rational humans would put in the same category as being water-boarded.

Caves are where Thai football coaches take their young teams for some unfathomable reason. When a dozen young Thai footballers were rescued in 2018, many people proclaimed that a miracle had taken place. The first movie about it, announced the same day as the last boy reappeared, is to be produced by a Christian film company. No surprises there. Just why it was thought to be a miracle is unclear for a few reasons.

Firstly, if God performed a miracle to get them out, why did he put them in there?

Secondly, the people physically responsible for actually getting them out, including all those who arrived to offer practical help, included professional divers (dozens), navy seals (tens), professional spelunkers (lots), geologists and cave experts (quite a few), Elon Musks (one), and alleged pedophiles (number uncertain). Preachers, imams, rabbis, priests (zero - thoughts and prayers don't register on the practical help scale), Jesus Christs (zero), saints (zero). In other words, no miracle workers were involved, in any way, in the actual rescue.

Thirdly, everybody knows that miracles stopped happening around the time of the invention of the video camera.

The Black Zones - 1/10 (some people like them)

THE WINDY ZONES

Hurricanes and tornadoes, like earthquakes and volcanoes, would be capricious and evil were they a deliberate design feature of a planet created for humans.

A certain amount of atmospheric circulation is necessary for many reasons including the spreading of seeds, redistribution of moisture and the avoidance of stagnation. But what reason is there for creating wind velocities that result in the mass destruction of buildings, trees and infrastructure and the deaths of thousands of humans and other animals? Couldn't the planet function as a place for humans to live without such catastrophic events?

As with deadly fire seasons, many otherwise lovely places have deadly wind seasons. If you look at a map of the 48 contiguous states of the USA, and imagine it divided into five vertical slices, the middle slice represents an area known as Tornado Alley. North Dakota, South Dakota, Iowa, Nebraska, Kansas, Oklahoma and Texas are the seven states that get 90% of all the tornadoes that hit the USA. If you live in a trailer park in one of these states, your chances of being killed by a tornado are eight thousand times higher than for any other human being. This is because tornados are attracted to trailer parks. The reason that there are so many trailer parks in Tornado Alley is because that's where people end up living after their houses get blown away. Insurance assessors usually reject claims for tornado damage invoking the Act of God clause, arguing that it overrides the specific tornado clause that the home owner paid extra to have included in their policy.

Drone footage on TV news is not always illuminating as to the type of neighborhood that's been destroyed because after a tornado's been through, it pretty much always looks like it was a trailer park that got hit.

Tornadoes usually hit during late spring, which might seem like a good time for alley dwellers to go on vacation, but there'd always be the risk of returning home to find that someone's parked a double-wide on the empty lot where your home used to be.

There's a secondary magnetic zone for tornadoes called Dixie Alley, which is the area along the Gulf Coast. Tornadoes usually occur there in the late fall. Which is not so good, because then you have to find another trailer in winter rather than in summer as is the case when your trailer picks a fine time to leave you in Kansas for example.

Tornadoes are rated according to the Enhanced Fujita Damage Intensity Scale which ranges from EF-0 to EF-5. An EF-1 is sufficient to strip the roof off a house or overturn a mobile home, even one with wind-deflecting modesty skirts, so an EF-5 is the meteorological equivalent of a Marshall stack that goes all the way to 12.

Violent tornadoes, meaning those of EF-3 or stronger only rarely occur anywhere outside Tornado Alley. Fortunately, even there, 95% of all tornadoes are below EF-3, and 80% are fart-in-a-bathtub EF-1 or 0. The 5% of serious ball busters of EF-3 and above are still a cause for concern because there are about a thousand tornadoes every year (seriously, who'd live there?) meaning there'll be about twenty totally destructive wind events, of biblical intensity, occurring at the rate of one every three or four days during the season.

Tornado Alley is also home to the world famous Tournedo Alley, a ten-lane Bowl-a-Rama Grill-House with a reputation for serving some of the finest cuts of sizzling lean beef anywhere on the I-35, just south of Purcell, Oklahoma.

Florida is more like an appendage than an alley, but it's the place that gets the leftover tornadoes when the alleys have had a gutsfull. The upside to the wet Florida type of tornado is that they tend to be weaker on average than the alley variety.

A step down from tornadoes and hurricanes are strong winds. Winds that blow so regularly and so annoyingly that they have acquired a name. There are well over a hundred of them.

They include the Bora, the Brickfielder, the Chinook, the Föhn, the Halny, the Hamsin, the Harmattan, the Mistral, the

Santa Ana and the Sirocco. Wind names sound sexy and fast so car manufacturers name cars after them. VW has Bora, Jetta, Passat and Sirocco. Maserati has Ghibli, Khamsin, Shamal, Mistral and Levante. Pagani has Zonda and Huayra and Lamborghini has Diablo and Huracan.

Ford retired the Zephyr name after noted Norwegian motoring journalist Jeremy Kverksonsen said the car very much deserved its name. "The Zephyr performed like the gentle breeze it was named after, a puff so mild that if it were a fart it would pass your cheeks without causing so much as a soft buttskin ripple, without a hint of a parp, and would not be smelt even by he who dealt it. Driving a Zephyr is as memorable as the 27th time you shat your nappy."

The Maestro was a model shared by the Austin, Morris and MG brands, but was neither rapid like the wind it was purportedly named after nor masterful in any way.

Australia's home grown manufacturer thankfully resisted any temptation to release either a Holden Brickfielder or a Holden Fremantle Doctor.

South Africa has its own equivalent of the Fremantle Doctor in the Cape Doctor, but both sound more like evil villains who extract teeth and perform other forms of surgical torture for gang bosses, Nazis and oligarchs, than good names for cars.

Intolerably windy places often get a regular battering from winds created by their local geography. Wellington, New

Zealand is such a place. The roaring forties get funneled into, and accelerated by, the gap between the North and South Island, before being blasted into the city. Locals are usually in denial about how windy it really is, often telling visitors they're just unlucky to be there on a particularly windy day. Some people have visited Wellington dozens of times and been unlucky enough to have struck a windy day on 96% of those visits.

Further evidence as to the nature of Wellington's breezy airs are the near horizontal trees on the surrounding hills, the numerous YouTube videos of aircraft trying to land while being blown sideways at Wellington Airport, and the name of the local rugby franchise, the Hurricanes. The wind at Wellington Airport averages 29km/h. Chicago, known in America as The Windy City, averages just 18km/h.

Umbrellas in Wellington have a life expectancy of less than two days because of the strong gusts that whistle up Cuba Street from the middle of the fearsomely chilly Cook Straight, which was the scene of the wind-induced capsize of the inter-island ferry Wahine, a six-decked vessel with a capacity of a thousand passengers and 200 cars, that resulted in the loss of 51 lives.

Summer in the otherwise perfectly sublime south of France, can be blighted by the Mistral, which blasts down the Rhône Valley, chilling, annoying and exhausting all those in its path before spreading across the delta of the Camargue, and petering out over the Mediterranean, though sometimes it persists all the way across Corsica and Sardinia.

The Mistral usually blows for a few days, sometimes a week or so, and is thankfully more common in spring and winter, when you're unlikely to be in its path. Unless you live there.

The Mistral blows strongly on an average of 100 days per year, and less strongly for 83 days, leaving just 182 days without noticeable wind. The tourism gurus extoll the virtues of the Mistral by saying it's responsible for the beautiful clear skies of Provence, and the official tourism website for Saint-Rémy-de-Provence proclaims that St Rémy is bathed in sunshine for more than 300 days a year.

A strong wind that lasts for more than a few hours is tiresome to say the least. Even if you're inside, the sound of a howling wind, rattling and shaking the house is enough to make otherwise sane people pray for it to stop. When extended prayer has no effect, people sometimes veer even further from sanity and start looking at their neighbors with suspicion, sometimes openly accusing them of praying for it to continue.

The infamous Saint-Rémy-de-Provence Pray-Off of 1889 occurred for exactly this reason. Following a harrowing wind-blown journey on the 8th of May 1889, Vincent Van Gogh arrived in St Rémy with Reverend Frederic Salles, the Pastor of the Reformed Protestant church in Arles. Pastor Salles saw Van Gogh safely into his new residence at the asylum known as the Monastere St Paul de Mausole, and proceeded to take a stroll around the town.

Local Catholics had been praying for three days for relief from the Mistral at the Collégiale Saint Martin, a monumental hulk built in 1821 on the site of a mediaeval church which had collapsed three years earlier, following an extended period of heavy windage. On seeing the protestant Pastor Salles sashaying by, two Catholics flew into a rage. The Pastor was lucky to escape a severe beating, or possibly a session with the iron maiden, as, perchance, a protestant youth group was passing by at the same time. Despite his protestations, the protestant Pastor was accused of being in the town to maliciously cause havoc by praying for the Mistral to bring damage and destruction to St Rémy.

As the numbers of protestant youth swelled around him, Pastor Salles was emboldened to meet the challenge head on and encouraged his flock to pray hard for the Mistral to continue in order to teach the filthy Catholics a lesson they'd not soon forget. Pastor Salles and his hard praying herd occupied the town square across from the Collégiale Saint Martin, and Catholics spilled out from the church kneeling down en masse to face them. The Pray-Off was on.

One hundred and eighty-five soldiers of God, on their knees, facing off, praying their hardest to prove whose God was greatest. If it occurred to any of them that they were all praying to the same God, they found a way, through prayer, to convince themselves that it was still a good idea to continue praying.

After 56 hours, the Mistral suddenly died. The Catholics cheered and headed to Murphy's Irish Bar to celebrate their victory. The Protestants skulked off in defeat. Pastor Salles returned promptly to Arles, admitting some years later that he'd fallen asleep just before the wind subsided.

The letter that Salles subsequently wrote to Van Gogh's brother Theo, about his trip to St Rémy with Vincent, unsurprisingly contains no mention of this embarrassing incident.

Also silent on the topic of the famous St Rémy Pray-Off of 1889 was one Michael de Nostredame, aka Nostradamus, who was born in St Rémy in 1503, and had absolutely no excuse not to see it coming.

All of which taken together sounds like an extreme dissing of one of the loveliest places on earth. But it shouldn't be taken that way, merely as further evidence that if the planet was designed for us, then the creator can't even make the best places fault free. One day you're enjoying the delights of a blissful summer holiday and the next your walk to the boulangerie for a baguette or two is as exhausting as Ronald Andersonsen's 99-day trek to and from the south pole.

Wind is responsible for many things, almost all of them not positive. Such as Hurricane Maria which made it clear to residents of Puerto Rico that their American citizenship could be effectively blown away by a combination of wind and a windbag, racist president.

Another bad thing about wind is wind chill which can be especially noticeable in cities. One can be enjoying a sunny stroll then, on reaching the end of the block and turning the corner, one is instantly shivering from a combination of shade and breeze. Effectively two different climates, ideally requiring different layers of clothing, within feet of each other. Not a very intelligent design, when compared with the far more gradual temperature changes found in a fishy environment:

San Francisco, however, must take the prize for instantaneous climate change. Although wind isn't the primary culprit in this case. It's fog. It's horribly common and the effect is worse than chilling. It's freezing. Tourists are often stunned to find that when they walk out of a shop or bar in the late afternoon, after just a short time inside, they feel like they've stepped into the freezer in a butcher's shop.

The fog rolls in from the ocean, engulfing the Golden Gate Bridge like an ominous, evil spirit in a horror movie, and its arrival in the city is so sudden, the temperature drop so great, that some tourists go into a state of shock. This happens in summer. Right through summer. No such thing as a nice warm evening in SF. One minute, shorts and t-shirt are comfortable, next minute, long johns, a onesie and a beanie jacket are essential.

The largest selling items in Bay Area novelty stores are space blankets, which visitors buy in order to get back to their hotels without getting hypothermia. A drone shot from 2000ft would show hordes of huddled, shiny silver creatures scurrying towards their hotels. Or at least it would if the camera could see through the fog.

Which is not to say that the Bay Area isn't a great place. It's wonderful. A fantastic part of the world. But a little design tweak to that fog thing could make it so much better. Three or four days a year perhaps, for the benefit of photographers, would be plenty.

The Windy Zones - 0/10 (while the wind blows)

THE CODE RED ZONES

The Code Red Zones are places unsuitable for human habitation on account of bombs and bullets and land mines and gas and biological weapons and anything else that evil bastards can think up as ways to kill and terrify other humans.

While there are still far more of these places around the planet than people should have to endure, Stephen Pinker makes a good case that there are a lot less of them than there used to be, and they occupy a lot less territory.

Which seems plausible as Spain is now a place where nobody expects the noble priests and soldiers of the Spanish Inquisition to smash down your door and drag you away to be tortured for the crime of not being sufficiently submissive to the sociopaths currently in power.

While it can still be dangerous to be black in America, it's not as dangerous as it used to be. As long as you avoid contact with the police. Which isn't always possible as it's sometimes necessary to leave the house for food and supplies or to go to work. Driving while black is still significantly more perilous than driving while white. But even if you stay home, police have been known to smash down the door of the wrong house and shoot the innocent occupants. Racially-motivated verbal and physical abuse and lynching of black people is no longer acceptable in the USA, or at least it wasn't for a period leading up to 2017.

Syria, Iraq, Afghanistan, Nigeria, Sudan, South Sudan, Pakistan, Ukraine, Somalia, Palestine, Libya and Yemen are currently among the places most unlikely to facilitate a peaceful family existence.

Not so long ago, the most dangerous places included London, France, Germany, Russia, Hiroshima and Nagasaki.

Cambodia used to be dangerous on account of falling bombs, napalm and agent orange. Most of that danger has passed, although the effects of agent orange and land mines are still a blight on far too many people. Now, on account of the country being run effectively as a mafia state, the most dangerous place for a poor person to be in Cambodia, is on a piece of land that a rich person wants.

In terms of mafia states, Russia's another place that can be dangerous, especially for journalists, politicians or others critical of the current gangster regime.

It could be argued that human endangerment and suffering caused by other humans shouldn't really be used to critique the design of the planet, but because it's claimed that the same creator is responsible for both the planet and the nasty, sociopathic end of the human behavior spectrum that causes all the misery, it's all part of the same thing.

Some combination of greed, stupidity and mental incapacity might at some time result in a major nuclear conflict, which could tip the balance into transforming most if not all of the planet into a Code Red Zone. It's not beyond the realms of possibility that we could make Antarctica the most habitable place on the planet.

The Code Red Zones - 0/10

THE KILLING ZONES

The Killing Zones are a lot like the Code Red Zones, but in this case they're zones where there are naturally occurring things, other than other humans, that endanger humans. Things like animals, plants, insects, bacteria and viruses.

If the designer wanted to make a creature that lived in a world that was not too boringly perfect, she could have designed a few things that were a wee bit on the dangerous side that we should learn to avoid. But there are literally thousands of things that naturally occur on planet earth that are capable of killing us.

We sapiens may think we've risen to the top of the food chain, but there are a lot of things out there that either haven't heard of that idea or really don't give a shit.

Insects for instance. Not all insects have the ability or inclination to kill us. Some are even useful to us, such as bees when they make our honey. But sometimes they decide to sting us, which can be fatal for some people. Probably not the best example of a benign insect.

Insects can be organized into three categories -

No Problem, Nuisance, and Dangerous Killers. Of course there'll be overlap, as in the first example, bees.

Bees are no problem, useful even, when they're pollinating flowers and fruit trees.

Bees are a nuisance, when they're inside your car, especially three or four of them, and you're in the fast lane, and you've been drinking, and you're not sure if it's the edibles that are making this whole thing seem way more terrifying than it really should be. Are they even real? Hard to say. Maybe if I turn up the music they'll go away. Whoa that was close. Shit, I really shouldn't be driving this fast.

And bees are dangerous killers, but only for the minority of people who are actually, medically allergic to being stung as opposed to the rest of us who just don't like being stung.

The nuisance example above may overlap into the dangerous killer example if the bees are in fact real and one of them stings the drunken stoner in the eye causing him to have a huge wreck with multiple fatalities. There are no official statistics on car crashes caused by bees, but there should be.

There's nothing to be learnt by dwelling on the No Problem category, but it's worth having a think about just how many Nuisance and Dangerous Killer creepy crawlers the designer thought would be interesting for us to have to deal with.

Termites - Major nuisance.

Lice - Yuk. Not individually dangerous but can transmit diseases.

Deer Ticks - Their bites can give you Lyme disease.

Wasps - Bees' idiot cousins that go to the pub solely to get drunk, smash glasses and punch people.

Black Widow Spiders - Death is a real possibility if you cross one.

Cockroaches - Yuk again. Serious nuisance. Can carry disease.

Parasitic worms - They live inside you and make you sick.

Bed bugs - They bite. Arguably harder to kill than cockroaches.

Centipedes - Some of them bite. Can cause serious infection. Not technically insects, but so what.

Assassin bugs - Infect people with Chagas disease.

Bullet ants - Reputedly their bite is as painful as being shot. The pain lasts for a whole day. That's 24 hours of chugging cheap whiskey and biting hard on a thick piece of leather or a stick. More painful than a gut shot? Nah. Couldn't be. Nothing's more painful than a gut shot.

Brazilian Wandering Spiders - The most venomous spiders in the world.

Mosquitos - These little malaria toting bastards have killed more people than all mad dictators put together.

Rat Fleas - If the Bubonic plague isn't enough to make you wonder why these guys were ever created, they also serve as carriers for tapeworms.

Africanized Honey Bees - aka Killer Bees. Yep, they kill people, even those without allergies by attacking en masse like old-time cannon fodder, except they face no cannons.

Regular Fleas - Not as bad as rat fleas, but they do dish out really annoying itchy bites and they're also disease carriers.

Fire Ants - Nasty biting little bastards. Cause sickness and sometimes even death.

Tsetse Flies - Nasty flying, biting, blood-sucking bastards that transmit a disease called sleeping sickness, which is a parasitic infection that involves headaches, fever, joint pain, itchiness, serious neurological problems, and death. Thousands of deaths every year. They're the insect equivalent of an A10 Warthog, which is basically just a flying gun. The proboscis of the tsetse fly even looks like an A10 nose cannon, and is used to similar effect.

The tsetse fly of course doesn't fire large, depleted uranium, armor-piercing shells at a rate of over 60 per second, so after it's killed you it won't continue to cause radiation linked illness, disease and birth defects among people in the vicinity for generations to come.

Horse Flies - Nasty flying, biting, blood-sucking bastards.

Sandflies - Smaller version of the above. The little bastards attack en masse, sometimes leaving bites that take months to disappear.

This list could go on and on and on but the question is, why would a creator make so many little buggy creatures that make human life either less pleasant, seriously annoying, extremely painful or even kill us? What sort of "working in mysterious ways" plan could it be part of?

What was the thought process of the creator? To make life challenging, there shall be annoying insects. Maybe even some dangerous insects. How about killer bees? Now we're talking. How about thousands of different insects capable of inflicting disease, misery and death? Woo hoo!

For a planet supposedly created specifically for human habitation, thousands of species of unpleasant bugs are a questionable design feature.

But bugs are just the beginning. Many plants are poisonous to humans. Apart from the need to provide murderers with a handy potion for spiking an adversary's meal, what was the creator thinking? Humans are omnivores, meaning those of us with adventurous palettes will try almost anything if it's recommended by someone we trust, or someone famous on the TV. Or Instagram.

Young humans don't need a recommendation. They're happy to try eating things like mud, Lego bricks, buttons and small batteries. A toddler left sitting next to a poisonous plant has a better than even chance of committing suicide. Most adult humans are smarter than that, but to get the ball rolling, back in the deep, distant past, someone had to be the first human to taste salmon, raccoon, carrots, fennel, rat, mushrooms and jalapeños, presumably not all at the same time.

The large number and variety of deadly plants ready and able to kill unwary humans, may seem incongruous with a supposedly benign planet.

To some nimble-fingered craft workers, hemlock may sound like a technique to avoid fraying around the bottom of a kaftan or pair of bellbottoms. But to most of us it sounds like a poison in an old time story. Which it is. Socrates was executed with it for the crime of being considerably more intelligent than the idiots around him. Ingestion of hemlock results in ascending muscular paralysis, which, just as it sounds, means the toes and feet go numb first, then the legs, then the torso and of course when your lungs go numb and fail to function it's goodnight.

Water hemlock is of the same family. If you yank one out of the ground you may mistake the root for an edible plant such as a parsnip, but that would be your last mistake. Actually, that's not correct. Eating it would be your last mistake. The effects are quick. Cows that eat water hemlock often die within fifteen minutes. Fifteen minutes of agony involving nausea, abdominal pain, respiratory impairment, kidney failure, irregular heartbeat, tremors, and seizures. If you don't eat enough to die, chances are you'll be permanently afflicted by tremors and amnesia. Which is especially cruel as you won't remember not to eat it should you survive and subsequently encounter it once more.

White snakeroot is a boringly normal looking weed so toxic that you don't even have to go near it for it to kill you. Thousands of people, including Abraham Lincoln's mother, died in the early 19th century from "milk sickness" or "milk poisoning". Unlike water hemlock, which kills cows quick smart, the toxins in white snakeroot pass into the cow and kill those who eat the cow's meat or drink her milk. A design of extreme dastardliness.

The pretty flowers of the oleander disguise the fact that every single part of this botanical murderer, leaves, flowers and fruit, contains poison. They're commonly found in gardens and parks, and are especially popular in the southern states of the USA, where many teenage mothers plant them after being forced by local evangelicals to give birth to their rapist's baby.

Aconitum, also known as monkshood, wolfsbane, or devil's helmet, is interestingly named as monks, wolves and devils occupy the same part in each nominal variation. Aconitum is used in poison-tipped arrows and spears. We can only surmise how the technique was discovered and perfected. Undoubtedly it would have involved an amount of trial and error and an amount of death and pain, both for developers and experimental subjects.

Castor oil is the product of processed castor beans. It was regularly administered by mothers to reluctant children in the 1950s as a health supplement, but was mostly useful as a laxative, as constipation was a side effect of the crappy diets common back then. Castor beans contain ricin which does a lot more than just give you the shits. Just a few beans are enough to kill in the agonizing manner common to many poisons which includes vomiting, diarrhea, seizures, cramps and spasms.

Although most deaths by castor bean involve inquisitive children and pets, ricin is also popular for killing pesky journalists, such as Georgi Markov, who was famously dispatched with a "Bulgarian umbrella" on Waterloo Bridge in London on the 7th of September 1978. Markov's murder was thought to be a birthday present for Bulgarian State Council chairman Todor Zhivkov, who had often been the target of Markov's criticism.

Assassination has long been a traditional birthday gift for despots in lands to the east of Europe, although ricin is not a compulsory ingredient. One of Vladimir Putin's birthday presents on 7 October 2006, was the execution of Russian journalist Anna Politkovskaya, who was gunned down in the elevator of her apartment block in central Moscow.

The Bulgarian Secret Service were not always successful in their umbrella-themed assassination attempts. Dissident journalist Vladimir Kostov discovered the cost of criticizing the Bulgarian regime in 2006 when he was attacked with a ricin-tipped Bulgarian umbrella in the Paris Metro. Kostov survived.

The Bulgarian umbrella looks like a normal umbrella but has a hidden pneumatic mechanism capable of shooting a ricin-loaded, pinhead-sized pellet from its tip with sufficient force to embed it deep into human flesh.

The Bulgarian umbrella should not be confused with ultra-luxury Bvlgarian umbrellas, most of which are not equipped with a ricin pellet delivery device, despite prices that range between eight and twelve thousand dollars. Only the top of the range Bvlgari Serpenti edition with the bejeweled snake head handle comes with the Ricinassassin device as standard. It also comes with an eye-watering thirty-four-thousand-dollar price tag, pellets not included. The Bvlgari Bvlgari Boutros Boutros Gali is not a real thing, although the Bvlgari Bvlgari Man Manbag is.

The Bulgarian umbrella was developed for the Bulgarian Secret Service by their genius inventor, R, who is not generally credited with having invented the automotive passenger ejector seat, but did in fact install one in a Lada for the Bulgarian Secret Service's allied agents of evil, the KGB, four years before Q installed the far more famous one in James Bond's golden Aston Martin DB5.

R is probably happy that his version is overlooked by most published works on espionage technology because its one and only deployment in the field was an abject failure.

When the KGB agent driving the Lada flipped the knob on the gear lever and pressed the button, 005 and the passenger seat were together catapulted through the simultaneously opening roof hatch. However unlike Q's more successful design, which jettisoned the roof hatch clear of the DB5, R's roof hatch flipped open, but remained attached to the car by the hinges on its rear edge. The design was thought to have been modified from R's original plan for economic reasons, as the comptroller of the KGB hated the idea of discarding a perfectly good roof hatch that could easily be retained for subsequent deployments.

As 005's surprised visage appeared above the roof line of the Lada, the KGB vehicle slowed abruptly with the vertical hatch lid now acting as a large air-brake against which the puny 1198cc Lada engine immediately struggled.

(The claimed 0-60mph time for a brand new Lada 1200 was a tortoise-like 25 seconds, which was always thought to be an optimistic claim by motoring journalists, although it was never independently tested as nobody could stay awake long enough to find out. The KGB Lada fitted with the ejector seat had already been around the clock twice, rarely fired on all four cylinders, and weighed almost twice as much as an example without the espionage equipment. The trunk-mounted, rear-facing machine guns alone weighed over 200Kg (440lbs) with full magazines.)

The propulsion unit on the base of the Lada's ejector seat had also been downgraded for reasons of economy and so it lacked sufficient thrust to launch the British agent far enough into the air to clear the upright hatch cover. Thus he fell straight back down into the spot he had recently vacated, much to the surprise of the KGB agent behind the wheel. 005's lightning fast reactions and advanced martial arts skills allowed him to quickly break the KGB agent's neck with a karate chop, kick him out through the driver's door (in every way a more economic technique than the ejector seat), and leap into the driver's seat to effect his getaway.

The Bulgarian Ejector Seat, as it became known to condescending KGB thugs, was never again used in the field. Neither was 005, who died in a hail of gunfire a short distance down the road, his getaway hampered by his inability to close the jammed ejector hatch, thus restricting the already lethargic Lada to a top speed of 18mph (29km/h).

On August 14th 1981, CIA double agent Boris Korczak was shopping at Giant Food Store in Vienna, Virginia when he was shot with a pellet gun by undercover KGB agent, Busta Nutzak. It's still unknown whether a Bulgarian umbrella was the disguise of choice for the KGB weapon as Nutzak has never publicly commented on the incident and the weather on the day, whilst cloudy, was mostly dry. Korczak did not recall seeing either Nutzak or an umbrella in the shop that day.

It may seem unusual to use the phrase, "luckily he was shot in the sweetbreads", as in most cases that'd likely be damn near as painful as a gut shot, but in this case it's true. Korczak reported that he thought he'd been stung by a bee. The ricin loaded pellet was about the size of the head of a small pin. The pellet lodged in Korczak's left kidney bean, which contained the poison and stopped it spreading to other parts of his body. Korczak's kidney sak treated the pellet as if it were a kidney stone and expelled it in the usual way, thus conferring on Korczak the unique position of being the only human to have ever pissed ricin and lived to tell the tale.

Korczak had been such a successful double agent that he'd risen to the rank of Major in the KGB, a rank that came with a decent salary, but one that he wasn't allowed to keep as he was deemed to be earning the wage in his capacity as an employee of the CIA. This was not his only beef with his Chief of Station however, as it was during a reception held at the Soviet Embassy in Copenhagen, Denmark in November 1979 that Korczak's boss nailed a few too many vodka shots and blew his cover.

Robert E Beauregard Stanley III was known for three things. His braggadocios behavior, his inability to hold his liquor, and his overwhelming stupidity. Alone, he would not have passed the entrance test for janitorial services at Langley, but money talks in all branches of government, so his powerful family saw to it that he rose quickly through the ranks of the CIA. It had been calculated by his superiors that he wouldn't be able to do a huge amount of damage sitting behind a desk in Copenhagen, but that calculation proved to be incorrect.

Believing he was being taunted by a KGB officer at the Soviet reception, Bobby "No Regard" Stanley, laughed in the KGB officer's face as he told him that one of his top agents, Major Boris Korczak, was, and always had been a CIA agent. Stanley's defense when confronted with this huge intelligence blunder was that it never happened, as he had absolutely no recall of the conversation. The no recall part was almost certainly true given how many vodka shots he'd nailed at the reception, on top of the "more than a few brewskis" he'd downed with Timmy, Squi and PJ earlier that afternoon.

When Stanley learned that he was likely to spend the rest of his CIA career in a basement at Langley, he immediately retired to the family estate near Selma, Alabama. Stanley swore that vodka would never again pass his lips, but he apparently failed to keep his word one last time as his body was found face down in a pool of vomit surrounded by empty liquor bottles, two of which were Stolichnaya. Police found no evidence of foul play although Sergeant Dan McClatchy commented, off the record, that there was plenty of evidence of foul behavior.

But back to deadly plants. If you eat too many tobacco leaves you'll die. Same thing happens if you smoke too many of 'em. While not usually thought of as a poison, tobacco kills more than 5 million people every year, so it would probably take the prize for most successful poisonous plant should the Shurdington Psychopath Association decide to award one.

Milquetoast Belladonna should not to be confused with Milquetoast Primadonna, the famous Swiss ballerina mercilessly lampooned by animators in the Wacky Races series. Milquetoast Belladonna is often mistaken for celery, and has the effect of bleaching the skin, disfiguring the face, especially the nose, and encouraging an excessive reliance on a cocktail of hard drugs supplied by compliant, irresponsible doctors, ultimately resulting in death.

The list could go on and on. In fact, Wikipedia lists over 130 poisonous plants, but the list doesn't claim to be anywhere near comprehensive as it's prefaced by a statement that the number of poisonous plants is "countless". Botanists tell us that plants are poisonous in order to deter consumption by herbivores and omnivores, but wouldn't a caring creator have settled for just making them taste really, really bad? Without them having to kill us?

Reading the Wikipedia list in detail should be avoided as it may cause the reader to become afflicted with Howard Hughes Disease, a condition which consigns the sufferer to a life indoors, due to an overwhelming fear of fatal flora.

It's a little known fact that shortly before becoming a recluse, Hughes visited the City Lights bookstore in San Francisco and purchased a book entitled Killer Weed: An Illustrated Dictionary of Poisonous Plants by Dudley J Pankhurst. It was Hughes last visit to any bookstore or in fact his last visit to any anything.

Frank William Gay, (aka Wild Billy), leader of the "Mormon Mafia" that comprised Hughes's inner circle in his later life, said the book purchase was a real tragedy as Hughes had been in a hurry and had failed to read the subtitle, which appeared on the cover in a much smaller font than the title. He had been hoping to find a book to help him in his efforts to grow killer chronic hydroponic marijuana in his Las Vegas penthouse. Billy Gay said that Hughes became engrossed in the book, reading it from cover to cover without a break. When he finally put the book down he was a changed man.

It was while the eccentric billionaire was eating his first meal after finishing Killer Weed, that Wild Billy Gay noticed Hughes closely inspecting his peas, one by one. It has been reported that Hughes obsessively sorted his peas by size (right down to designing a special fork for the purpose) owing to his increasingly debilitating OCD, but the real reason he played with his food in this way was to ensure that every morsel entering his mouth was not the spawn of a poisonous plant.

Although Hughes' death was recorded as due to kidney failure, the examining doctor initially suspected foul play.

Hughes' body was seriously malnourished, a pale, unrecognizable shadow of his former self, measuring 6ft 4in (193cm) in length (being post mortem jargon for height) but weighing in at just 90lb (41kg). The five broken hypodermic needles embedded in his arms were not deemed to be suspicious as Hughes was known to have been injecting himself with codeine for many years. Ironically, Hughes final demise was caused by Milquetoast Belladonna poisoning, an honest mistake made by his personal chef, Constantine Toblerone, who served a year's penance in a Mormon tabernacle before resurrecting his career and going on to become personal chef for Michael Jackson many years later.

Some toadstools may be about the right size and shape for a toad to use as a backless chair, but no mushroom is large enough to accommodate a race between teams of harnessed huskies.

Poisonous toadstools are sometimes mistaken for edible mushrooms, a mistake that can lead to serious illness and/or death. The Wikipedia list of deadly fungus species is "not exhaustive" but nevertheless still names about four dozen of the blighters. Interestingly, the deadly toxic agents in most species predominantly do their killing by attacking the liver or kidneys. What makes it interesting is that liver and kidneys, along with bacon and gravy are among the most delicious things to combine with mushrooms (of the non-poisonous variety), especially for breakfast after a big night.

Is the presence of four dozen species of poisonous fungi a good design feature, one of benefit to the human population of planet earth? Would a half dozen species not have been enough?

If you're lucky enough to survive the various poisons provided by plants and insects, you may be killed by any number of animals.

Scorpions are considered by some to be insects or arachnids rather than animals. For the purposes of this book it really doesn't matter. There are well over a thousand different species of scorpion but almost all of them are not poisonous enough to kill humans. Leaving just twenty-five species of scorpion responsible for between one and five thousand deaths each year. The wide range of the estimated number of deaths by scorpion is indicative of the fact that most scorpion victims live in very poor countries. Or at least very poor parts of mildly poor countries. Or lazy research.

Leopards kill about ten to twenty people in India each year. But the number is decreasing and will soon be zero unless serious measures are taken to cull the numbers of big game hunters in the wild, preferably to zero.

Lions generally prefer to munch on meat with a bit of fur on it, though they have been known on occasion to actively hunt humans, or fight back, as it should be more correctly described. One article on the internet, which exhibits all the signs of little to no research, estimates the number of people killed each year by lions at about seventy.

Tigers are the world champs of the big cat division when it comes to killing humans. Tens to hundreds each year is the estimate of the aforementioned website which has been nominated for a Webby in the category of "Least Time Wasted on Actual Research When Knocking Out a Clickbait Listicle". Tens to hundreds is another way of saying somewhere between 9 and 999. Nice work. Very Informative.

Wikipedia seems to be more academically rigorous. "The most comprehensive study of deaths due to tiger attacks estimates that at least 373,000 people died due to tiger attacks between 1800 and 2009, the majority of these attacks occurring in South and Southeast Asia. Over the last five centuries, an estimated one million people have been eaten by tigers." Holy shit!

The places humans are most likely to be killed by tigers are in parts of India, such as Kumaon, Garhwal, the Sundarbans, and Bengal, as well as in zoos, circuses, cages, and Las Vegas. Even though tigers usually avoid elephants, a case was reported, according to Wikipedia, in which a fatally wounded tiger attacked and killed the hunter who shot it, the hunter mistakenly assuming he was safe on the back of an elephant. Good work, tiger.

According to Roy Horn, of Siegfried and Roy fame, Montecore, a huge, seven-year-old male tiger, saved his life by attempting to drag him to safety after he suffered a stroke. None of the hundreds of people who witnessed the event agreed with Horn's account, and it's safe to say his recollection was clouded by the fact that he was critically injured, suffered serious blood loss and went into a state of shock during the Mauling at the Mirage. Horn may have also had a stroke before or as a result of the attack/rescue, but that was never unequivocally diagnosed.

When shown video of the event, David Hasselhoff disagreed with Horn's assessment, saying that even if Montecore had been carrying a red plastic thing and wearing a red Speedo, it wouldn't have looked anything like life saving as he understood it.

As a result of Montecore's amateur paramedic adventure, the Mirage was forced to close the Siegfried and Roy Show resulting in the loss of jobs for 267 people. "Montecore is a great cat," said Horn, three years later, when he'd finally relearned how to walk and talk, albeit with great difficulty, but it was finally accepted that the show was over permanently as the Las Vegas City Council deemed Roy's mauled face too distasteful to be allowed to appear on any billboard in Vegas, lest it scare the punters away to Reno.

Between one and a few hundred people are killed by cows every year. The real number is probably towards the lower end of that guess, as cows are not at all dangerous, unless you're foolish enough to try to shelter beneath one during a thunderstorm. Considering how many of them we kill each year, it's very lucky they're stupid, as there are more than enough of them to cause serious trouble were they to form a well regulated militia.

Forming a well regulated militia must be more difficult than it sounds as the most common result of a motivated band of trailer park residents getting together to form one, is that they end up accidentally shooting themselves and each other after a few hours of drinking moonshine around a campfire or burning cross.

Most deaths by horse (a smallish number is the statistical consensus) are accidents rather than premeditation on the horse's part. Horse related deaths that aren't accidents usually occur after some very small person has whipped the flank of a running horse, to which the horse has responded by trying to get the nuisance off its back, usually by rubbing it against the side of the horse running alongside.

Jockeys mostly die soon after making a horse jump over a tall hedge, although there is one recorded instance of a horse actually winning a race with a dead nuisance on his back, the little one having suffered a heart attack on the way.

Impalation is the technical term for being skewered on the antlers of an Impala or other antlered beast. It should not be confused with either being Gored (such as happened to Al, following the US presidential election of 2000) or being gored which is the term for what should ideally happen to every idiot who dresses up in white clothes with a red scarf and runs through narrow lanes in Spain.

A few hundred people are killed each year by deer, but not usually by impalation. It's almost always as a result of a deer suddenly appearing in the path of the victim's vehicle.

Wolves are one of the most attractive looking dog species on the planet, due to having been unmolested by breeders who seem hell bent on destroying future generations of mutts by trying to shorten their legs, scrunch up their faces, and generally make them look less and less viable as a species, all in the vain pursuit of a colored ribbon to hang on their wall. Wolves don't kill many humans.

Australia has dingoes instead of wolves. Dingoes hardly ever kill people, apart from babies, but they still often look at humans like they wouldn't mind a taste. If you need a trick to remember whether Australia has dingoes or wolves, just think of the colloquial ozzy phrase, "as dry as a dead dingo's donger," which would not work very well with the word "wolf". The phrase is generally used in response to the question, "Wanna beer, mate?" "Fuckin' oath. Me throat's as dry as a dead dingo's donger."

It's thought that the ancestors of all dogs were wolves, although the final verdict on this isn't yet in. When people think of death by domestic dog, it's generally imagined as local children having their faces ripped off by the pit bull that's been routinely beaten by the antisocial, dickhead loser from three doors down. While that scenario does occur far too often, along with the even more common scenario of pit bulls tearing off the faces of the owner's own children, statistically the number is very small when compared to the 25,000 - 30,000 people estimated to die each year after being bitten by a dog. In these deaths the dogs are only half to blame - the biting half. The dying half is more to do with rabies, which not only infects and kills humans, but also causes dogs to be far more in the mood to do a bit of biting. Most deaths by rabid dog occur in Asia

Other carriers of rabies are more statistically significant in the Americas and Europe. Rabid skunks and bats kill people there, though it's not very common, except among two small, offshoot Amish sects, who have a tradition of installing cribs for new born babies in the lower branches of trees, thus making them easy targets for rabid skunks and rabid bats alike. Followers of the cult believe that prayer can cure rabies in babies, but if they spent a bit more time learning about statistics and science rather than learning how to pray and raise a barn, they might discover that their infant mortality rate would be classified as genocide in most civilized communities.

Cape Buffaloes are like big angry cows. Or bald angry bison. Nobody knows for sure why they're so angry most of the time, but if you see one it's a very good idea to just walk away, whatever your name may be. They kill over 200 people every year. In parts of Africa where the Big Buffs are most common, the song Walk Away Renee by The Left Banke is played every morning as a cautionary reminder, while the children depart the morning assembly and sashay their way to their classrooms.

Surprisingly this repetition has not caused the song to be widely loathed, in fact the Left Banke, along with Sixto Rodriguez, have been in local pop charts continuously for over forty years in South Africa. Muzak researchers discovered that supermarkets where the song is played on high rotation had better sales numbers than where the song wasn't played at all.

The researchers took things a step further by testing just how much repeated old shit people could possibly endure while trying to buy food in the famous Muzak High Rotation Experiment of 2008 in the Mega Super Value Mart in Cape Town. The sound system was set to play just three songs on permanent rotation, Walk Away Renee, Sugar Man by Sixto Rodriguez, and some piece of shit by Abba (doesn't matter which one) occasionally interrupted with cheery advertisements which also included stings from the same songs.

The High Rotation Experiment had a much bigger effect than the researchers could possibly have imagined. Sales plummeted, but that's hardly surprising. It was the effect on the staff that took the researchers by surprise. Three weeks after the start of the experiment, the researchers arrived at the store to do some first hand observation of shoppers' habits and found the store looking as though it been hit by an earthquake.

As they got closer they realized it looked more like a battlefield, the epicenter of an intense, recently-concluded firefight. In terms of the recent conclusion of the firefight they were almost correct, but there was one last skirmish still to take place just before brigades of heavily armed police arrived on the scene.

As they made their way into the crumbling, smoldering store the researchers were ambushed by the Mega Super Value Mart staff, who may have initially been mistaken for a pack of rabid zombies, but who had, in fact, formed a well regulated militia. They'd equipped themselves with an array of firearms and blown away every Muzak speaker in the store, along with the amplification equipment and a lot more besides. When you've just unloaded an AK47 into a ceiling speaker, it's pretty hard to avoid the temptation of a fully stacked milk freezer.

Following the restoration of order by the police SWAT teams, paramedics had to call for the assistance of locally known circus strong man, Big Bill, in order to move the bodies of the researchers, such was the weight of lead that had been pumped into them by the gun-crazed shelf-stackers before they themselves were drilled by a hail of police bullets.

Next time you find yourself rushing to find what you need in order to effect a quick escape from shop speakers farting out some hideous piece of decades old pop muzak shite, you can take comfort in the thought that at least once, in far off Africa, the worst purveyors of this kind of aural pollution got their just desserts. As Toto almost said, there's nothing that a hundred men or more could ever do, I bless the drains down in Africa, especially for the blood of all those tone deaf cocksuckers that flowed down them.

Like most humans, most elephants are docile and friendly most of the time, but can be dangerous if sufficiently provoked. Or even mildly provoked after ten or more pints of lager. African villages have occasionally been seriously damaged and villagers killed and maimed by hordes of the rampaging, flesh and bone bulldozers, but as these events often occurred immediately following a cull of local elephant herds, it seems fair enough. Indian villages have sometimes copped the same treatment, the villagers reporting on a number of occasions that the elephants were drunk.

"There are travelers' tales from about 1839 reporting Zulu accounts that 'elephants gently warm their brains with fermented fruits,'" according to Steve Morris, a biologist at the University of Bristol, and there are a number of videos on YouTube of elephants who certainly look like they've been warming their brains with something. But not with naturally fermented alcohol from rotting marula fruit, as has been mostly surmised. Although Morris debunked the marula fruit theory, he's never commented on the theory that elephants have secret factories in which they produce elephant beer, a recipe stolen by employees of the Carlsberg Brewery while on safari in 1954.

The most recent alleged drunk elephant attack occurred in India in 2002, resulting in the deaths of six villagers, who were avenged by the killing of 200 elephants. Which might seem like overkill to some, although not to India's most prolific poacher who personally killed over 300 elephants, before himself being tracked down and killed by an operation involving 300 Indian policemen.

Elephants kill a few hundred people every year, but if humans keep killing elephants at the rate we do, that threat will disappear very soon.

Snakes kill about 100,000 people every year. How many of them are killed by us is not known, as snake deaths are not required to be notified to the department of records. We also don't care because it was a snake who struck up a conversation with Eve and caused us all no end of problems as a result. If it had just bitten her instead of trying to chat her up it would have saved us all a lot of bother.

Bulls are thought of as dangerous, but they don't kill anywhere near enough matadors, and should therefore be on the protected animals list.

Bears are also considered to be extremely dangerous, but in fact they're not dangerous enough because if that one in The

Revenant had killed the Leonardo DiCaprio character at the beginning when it should have, we would have all been spared the hideous boredom of sitting through that overlong piece of pretentious, stupid, implausible shit.

Crocodiles and alligators are nasty pieces of work, but they're not a serious problem as they generally only kill stupid people. The croc death toll is estimated to be between one and three thousand idiots per year. Not enough really.

Almost three thousand human deaths are attributed to the Fred Flintstone of African wildlife, the hippopotamus, which is considered by many to be Africa's most dangerous animal.

You can be killed by any of the aforementioned things without tempting fate by going in the water, but if you do that, there are dangers there as well.

When a shark swims just below the surface its ominous looking dorsal fin betrays its position. Some may think that a benevolent creator may have done this to give swimming humans a warning, and therefore time to get out of the water. Mostly it's a notification that you're about to be killed.

If you're any more than knee deep, you have to be really quick or really lucky. If you're swimming, meaning eyes pretty much at water level, the first time you spot a shark fin, it'll likely be about 10 meters (30feet) away. Can you make it out of the water in 10 seconds? That's a trick question. Doesn't matter. A shark can cover that distance in one second.

Jellyfish aren't normally thought of as killers, but they actually kill 15 to 30 times as many people as sharks do. Even if they don't kill you, the stings can really hurt and/or itch like crazy, and those little blue bottle things they have in Australia can even sting you after they're washed up dead on the beach.

If you survive all those things, there's a chance you'll fall prey to one of the micro-killers.

For every ton of humans on planet earth there are 1300 tons of bacteria. Bacterial cells are everywhere. Millions of them in every gram of soil, millions of them in every teaspoonful of water, billions or trillions of them in or on every living thing, in both symbiotic and parasitic relationships.

An average sized human consists of about 30 trillion human cells. An average sized human hosts about 39 trillion bacterial cells. Was planet earth designed for us to live on, or were we designed for bacteria to live on? And in? Unlike terrorist cells, not all bacterial cells are out to kill us. But some of them are, and it only takes a tiny percentage of billions or trillions to mean that there are lots of them.

Bacterial cells that aren't out to get us often perform useful functions such as recycling organic matter, otherwise known as turning dead bodies into rotting, putrid, gunk soup and then turning the resulting molecules back into things that can go around and be born again. They also assist in turning delicious food into disgusting, smelly, fecal matter inside our bodies.

Most bacteria associated with humans are the ones in our guts and on our skin. Lots of them are beneficial to the functioning of our systems, and lots of them aren't, but are rendered harmless by our immune systems. Which leaves the ones that are classified as pathogens, the ones that cause diseases. Their repertoire includes cholera, bubonic plague, leprosy, syphilis, tuberculosis, and many other infectious diseases which result in millions of deaths each year. A full list of infectious bacteria harmful to humans, but which reside on, in, or near us would resemble, and be as boring to read, as five pages of lorem ipsum. Antibiotics have proved effective (so far) in dealing with many of them, but the question remains, why would a creator design a world with so many devastating microbial killers? Would half a dozen not have been enough?

Bacteria on the skin is the cause of body odor which must have been a disgusting, but ever-present part of daily life for thousands of generations. Modern plumbing has given us the ability to deal with body odor, although it is a sad commentary on today's society that efficient showering facilities are apparently unavailable to at least one in four supermarket shelf stackers.

Apart from olfactory relief, the washing of human skin has other benefits. Notably pertaining to surgeons' hands. It is not certain at what point cleanliness acquired its place next to godliness, but it took science, rather than prayer, to introduce it as a health benefit. Surprisingly the concept of cleanliness in operating theatres has only been around for a hundred and fifty years. Before then, surgeons wouldn't bother to rinse the bone saw between amputations and often wiped their hands on a lab coat already sodden with the blood of a TB sufferer. In other words, humans have endured many thousands of years of disease and deprivation of opportunity to heal, because of a system originally created where dirt, infection and disease was an integral feature. Mysterious ways are one thing, but an overabundance of pathogens is downright pathological.

Viruses are nasty little things that may be smaller than bacteria but they're just as deadly. Viruses can infect all manner of life forms including humans, other animals, plants, and even bacteria. When they get inside the living cells of other organisms they replicate rapidly, which is usually bad news, and sometimes the worst news, assuming you weren't hoping to die.

Viruses hang about on street corners doing not much of anything until given the opportunity to get inside something which they then attempt to kill. Plant viruses jump on passing insects such as aphids, and some of the most deadly-to-human varieties hail a ride on various blood-sucking insects, often mosquitoes, the Uber of the virus world. They can also ride-share on small particles or droplets of flying snot produced by sneezes or small particles of flying phlegm produced by coughing. It's not pleasant to reflect on the thought of inhaling someone else's snot or phlegm, but it'd be unlikely to do you any harm, so long as it was virus free. Likewise, whenever you smell a fart, what's actually occurring is small airborne particles of poo are finding their way into your nasal passages and clinging on in there. That's what we identify as a smell. Again a very unpleasant thought, which should possibly have come with a trigger warning, but it's too late for that now. Fecal-oral transfer of viruses is not uncommon. Norovirus and rotavirus are transmitted in this way, although it usually occurs as a result of poor hygiene, rather than being caught in an elevator with an SBD (SBD is the technical term for a Silent But Deadly fart - deadly being hyperbole in most instances).

Sexual contact is also a common means of viral transmission, which seems like a particularly perverse concept when you consider that making the beast with two backs is essential for procreation, yet comes with the threat of a potentially deadly booby trap in many instances. The booby trap should not be confused with the honey trap; which is a long established method of gaining compromising information for blackmail purposes and takes many forms, always tailored to the predilections of the target, which may include hookers performing golden showers on Moscow hotel beds.

Smallpox, yellow fever, measles, influenza, dengue fever, typhus, plague, bubonic plague, cholera, malaria, meningitis,

HIV/AIDS, Ebola, SARS, and Zika could all spread like a wildfire given the right circumstances, causing epidemics and pandemics capable of killing millions of people. The reigning world champion of this division is the Spanish Flu which made the Spanish Inquisition look like a birthday party with fluffy kittens, by killing 75 million people between 1918 and 1920. The Spanish Flu may be dethroned at any time given the inevitable likelihood that new virus strains will continue to emerge.

It's difficult to understand why a caring creator might have created Spanish Flu.

A lot of people can happily live their whole lives without encountering smallpox, so why create smallpox? From humanity's point of view there's no upside to the pox ever having existed. The evidence for this is that it's been pretty much eradicated by scientific endeavor and there's no apparent downside. Despite this, there are still lunatics who hate vaccines so much that they'd prefer to see smallpox come back and once again ravage the planet. Perhaps a celebrity endorsed hemlock salad would appeal to them.

There are some things on our planet that are not inherently dangerous to smart people, but, like crocodiles, can be very dangerous to the not so bright.

Cliffs can be dangerous whether you're at the top or the bottom. You can fall from the top and die, or if you're at the bottom you can be struck and killed by a falling rock, or a falling rock climber.

If you fall from a cliff into a river, the water may break your fall, but then you may drown, or get bashed to pieces on the jagged rocks in the rapids just before the waterfall. Or the waterfall itself may kill you.

Even slopes can be deadly, particularly ones covered in shale or slippery mud. Once again there may be a river at the bottom of the slope. Or a cliff. And then a river.

Some slopes are made more deadly by silly ideas. Such as trying to win a rolling cheese by chasing it down a very steep hill. Despite what morons may think, the finishing line is not the best place to spectate from, as morons standing there would likely be knocked down and killed by one or more of the dozens of lunatics tumbling down the hill in pursuit of the cheese. Or by the cheese itself, which weighs around eight pounds, or three and a half kilos, and which packs a head-smashing punch as it reaches a terminal velocity in excess of the open road speed limit. The best part about the annual Cooper's Hill Cheese-Rolling and Wake in Gloucestershire is that no bulls or other animals are harmed in the event.

With one exception. A heat for animals was introduced in 1993, but was never repeated. The reason the animal event failed to catch on was that most animals, unlike their human counterparts, were too smart to voluntarily launch themselves down the ridiculously steep hill. Even mice refused to participate. The event was won by one of the four hedgehogs entered by the Shurdington Psychopath Association, who prodded the hogs until they curled up into balls and then kicked them down the slope. Unfortunately, the victorious hedgehog was unable to claim his cheese as he had to be scraped off the wall of a house on the other side of the road at the bottom of the hill.

A disappointing feature of recently held events is that despite large numbers of serious injuries, no participants have actually died, and therefore the opportunity for the wake component of the Cooper's Hill Cheese-Rolling and Wake, aka the grand finale drinking session, has had to be replaced by a drinking session without a name or official excuse.

There are literally thousands of creatures and other things here on our planet that have the real chance of seriously hurting us, or killing us, if we come into contact with them.

The Killing Zones - 0/10

THE GREEN ZONES

Mostly, the Green Zones are good places for humans to live, there being enough water to keep the plants growing, but not so much that learning to breath under water is a requirement.

Some Green Zones, however, are not ideal habitats for most humans, usually on account of being too fertile, thus turning into jungles. Some jungles have vegetation so thick that you can't move through them without swinging a sharp blade in front of you. Some are bounded by rivers with almost impenetrable borders of mangroves, making it extremely difficult to debark a canoe and enter the jungle, even if there are no crocodiles. A mangrove is either a type of tree that grows in water or a shady clearing amongst trees with a big screen TV, a pool table, a pinball machine, a fridge full of beer and a Lazy-boy recliner.

As well as having too many plants, jungles often have too many dangerous animals, and bugs, and snakes, including pythons big enough to swallow a man and his dog, and piranhas in the river which will treat your toes like chicken nibbles if you're foolish enough to try to step out of your canoe in order to battle your way through the mangroves.

In 1934 Edward J Tarvey, of the Staffordshire Tarveys, set out on an expedition up the Amazon river in an effort to combat corruption and bring law and order to the heart of the deepest, darkest part of the Amazonian Jungle. At least that was the reason publicly announced by Tarvey, whose mission was planned in almost indecent haste. There were rumors that he was in fact trying to avoid prosecution for crimes of fraud and embezzlement against his in-laws, as well as to escape a wife said to be prone to violent outbursts that often left Tarvey with blackened eyes and a swollen nose. Tarvey calculated that the family fraud scandal would blow over after a few years at which time he'd return as a hero adventurer. Or he'd die trying. He succeeded in neither.

Three days after setting off up the Amazon, Tarvey returned to the port city of Macapá near the river mouth. But he was not aboard his expedition boat, rather he was on a small river craft of local origin, and he was accompanied by just five of his starting crew of fifteen. Tarvey refused to comment on the circumstances surrounding the loss of his expedition boat and most of his crew, although it was fairly obvious to most that the infamous Amazonian river pirate, Ricardo Negrobarba, aka Blackbeard Ricky, had struck again.

Tarvey left Brazil almost immediately, but a gunboat was nevertheless sent up the river to investigate. The reason for

Tarvey's hasty departure soon became apparent when it was revealed that nine of the ten missing crew members were pirates, and the man Tarvey had hired to act as first mate was Ricardo Negrobarba himself, who had ingeniously disguised himself with a clean shaven face.

Adding to Tarvey's humiliation due to his lack of diligent preparation came the revelation that in his haste to put together his law and order mission, he'd not even begun to read the only reference material he'd taken with him, a copy of Rudyard Kipling's The Jungle Book. Tarvey knew it from school days, and believed it to contain many references to the Law of the Jungle.

One of the crew members who returned with Tarvey said that Negrobarba, who, surprisingly, had read Kipling's book, had mocked Tarvey by muttering "Rikki-Trikki-Tavi" under his breath whenever Tarvey turned his back on him. On the second day, Negrobarba's taunting became blatant, beginning in the morning when he changed it to "Ricky tickle Tarvey", accompanied by a quick tickling flick of Tarvey's rib cage, and further in the afternoon when he changed it to "Ricky takey Tarvey's boat", which finally caused Tarvey to aggressively confront him whereupon he found himself facing the pointy end of a cutlass.

This was also the moment that Tarvey noticed how quickly a dark shadow of heavy beard growth had begun to cover his first mate's face.

Tarvey did not return to Britain, instead disembarking in New York, where he initially struggled to survive, his embezzled funds now exhausted, but he eventually bagged a job in a travelling side show as a bearded lady, having grown a full set of whiskers and long hair, not only to disguise himself against creditors' agents, and humiliation, but also because he was too short on funds to afford proper grooming equipment.

After a spot more fraud and embezzlement, Tarvey changed his name to Edward J Kennedy, and was elected to the US Congress in the 12th District of Ohio, where he served for an extremely lucrative forty-three years. Reluctant to personally return to Britain, he nevertheless sent an agent to purchase his in-laws' family estate in 1969, on which he planned to build a jungle-themed theme park. The plan for the park was abandoned after three years of wrangling with the local council, and the estate returned to a state of natural wilderness, or the closest thing to a jungle to be found in Britain.

Many countries have experienced a rapid decline in jungle zones. Kenya's last pocket of tropical rainforest, the Kakamega Forest, once part of a jungle that stretched all the way across central Africa, now covers an area of less than 100 square miles.

Most of the Green Zones aren't jungles, which makes them the best places for humans to live.

Green Zones - 8/10

THE CONTINENTS

Having established that most of planet Earth is not a Goldilocks Zone, it's time to turn our attention to the wide variety of dry lands that do have the potential to support human life. These areas comprise a total of just 14.5% of the planet's surface, when oceans (71%), deserts (8.7%) and mountains (5.8%) are subtracted.

The dry bits of the earth's surface are separated by the aforementioned oceans, which is almost certainly a very good thing. Imagine the never-ending warfare if there weren't any naturally occurring moats to keep us apart. Whether they need to occupy quite such an extensive area is dubious at best.

An intelligent designer might have saved a lot of people a lot of grief if he'd put a reasonable amount of water between Israel and the rest of the Middle East. There's plenty of room for an Israel-sized island between Crete and Cyprus, although Cyprus demonstrates that a massive moat does not necessarily lead to peaceful co-existence. And just how a creator might have been able to put a body of water between Sunni and Shia is a much more difficult question.

For better or worse, the dividing oceans, and other physical features, have given us land masses that have been classified as continents. There's some disagreement about exactly how many there are and exactly where the dividing lines should be, but that doesn't really matter for a book as imprecise and unscientific as this one. The Sinai Peninsula, which is part of Egypt, is usually categorized as being part of Asia, along with Japan and Indonesia, while the rest of Egypt is part of Africa, which is once again, mostly not a lot like Egypt, and provides another reason not to take the established classifications too seriously.

THE AMERICAS

The American Continent occupies 28.4% of the land area of planet earth. It stretches all the way from the Arctic to pretty close to Antarctica so there's a huge variance in climate and geography, from a vast, frigid top end to really quite pleasant in the middle and back to way too cold.

It's thought that the first humans arrived from Asia between 40,000 and 17,000 years ago.

The first European settlement in the Americas was established by the Norse explorer Leif Ericson, known to his friends as Autumn, because of his reputation for being regularly blown off course. The location of Erikssen's first colony is believed to be somewhere in Newfoundland, but it is not known for certain, because, like an Autumn leaf, it failed to endure. Also, as Erikksonn found it by accident after being blown off course, there were no accurate navigational clues in the captain's log.

Prior to this, whilst travelling to Norway from Greenland in 999AD, Autumn Lief and crew were unsurprisingly blown off course, and, clearly confused as to their whereabouts, they spent the Summer in the Hebrides, possibly looking for locals

NOT VERY INTELLIGENT DESIGN TOO

to ask for directions. Whilst a pleasant time was apparently had by all, they eventually regretted the decision to tarry when it dawned on them that their journey to Norway would have to continue in the less pleasant conditions afforded by late Autumn and Winter.

On his arrival in Norway, Erikssen joined the court of King Olaf Tryggvason, who had recently been bjorn again, which necessitated Liefff's conversion to Christianity. Tryggvvasssensen then tasked Errrrikkkksensen with converting Greenlanders to Christianity and thus started him on the journey that would become his claim to fame.

Leif apparently saw Newfoundland for the first time, after being blown off course on his way to Greenland. He discovered wheat fields and, more excitingly, grape vines, which inspired him to initially name the place Vinland. It is unclear when the name was finally changed to Newfoundland, although it was known for various periods in the interim as Newvinland, Newfoundvinland and of course Newfoundvinlandland, which was much more in keeping with Norse naming traditions and would certainly have remained that way were it situated within cooee of Scandinavia.

Erikkssensen reportedly rescued two shipwrecked men, who were thus perhaps the first Europeans to set foot on the non-Greenland part of the American Continent, if there's any truth to the story. Who those men might have been or where they might have come from is a mystery. Autumn Lief then headed

NOT VERY INTELLIGENT DESIGN TOO

back to Greenland to get on with the conversion of the locals to Christianity.

At some point, Lief heard about Bjarni Herjólfsson, an intrepid Viking trader, who claimed to have been blown off course and seen land to the west of Greenland some years earlier, although strangely enough he didn't bother to actually set foot on that previously undiscovered land. Lief tracked Bjarney down and bought his ship, then set off, this time in a deliberate attempt to sail to the new world.

Erik the Red, Lieff's dad, was on his way to join the expedition, but fell off his horse, resulting in a painful bone spur, so he deferred his involvement. He also said it was a bad omen. This time Erikkssenn made it back to Newfoundland, and after a couple of false starts established a settlement called Leifsbudir, which of course didn't last very long.

A year or so later, towards the end of a heavy night of drinking with his so-called friends at the Viking Tavern in Iceland, Lief abruptly stood up and declared that he would smite with furious anger any man who dared call him Autumn again.

It was a fair call. The son of Erik the Red should not be ridiculed. Not as an adult anyway. Autumn had been ridiculed mercilessly as a schoolboy on account of his mother's name, Þjóðhildur, which Lief's class mates purposely mispronounced as pooholder.

As the Vikings glanced about amongst themselves to try to gauge the seriousness of Lief's threat, the door burst open and in walked Barney Harrelsonson, the merchant who'd sold Erikksen his ship. "Autumn," he cried. "I heard you were here in Iceland. Where were you trying to go before you got blown off course? Ha ha ha."

Eriksen pulled his axe from his belt, and smote Barney a hefty blow that severed his left arm. "Let that be a warning to all of you," he said. "If you steal my honor, I will take your hand so that you steal no more."

Lief Ericson was banished from Iceland on the basis of a court finding that his axe attack on Barney Harrellsson was "not a very Christian thing to do," and "there is no religious text recognized by Vikings that allows for the cutting off of body parts as punishment."

Autumn never returned to Iceland, or America, or anywhere else. It's presumed his ship was blown permanently off course as he was attempting to sail to Norway.

Many of the human inhabitants of North, South and Central America believe that the place they live is the greatest place on earth. Such beliefs are inherently subjective, which means they're equally correct. But they're also totally contradictory, meaning they can't be equally correct. Objectively, some places have to be better than others.

We'll take it from the top.

North America

Greenland doesn't really seem like part of America, but in terms of continental classification, it's generally agreed that it is. The latitude of Greenland disqualifies any part of it as a place any rational human being would be happy to live, so the only purpose it really serves is that of a large ice fishing hut made of dirt and rock.

Canada. It's hard to successfully argue that you live in the best country when everybody's scrunched up against the border. If the Canadian border wall wasn't there, the pressure would pretty much push everybody southward, and quite a few would end up splashing into some big lakes or rivers. Canada's like a stadium rock concert with a total attendance of one or two hundred people. A bunch of keen punters pressed hard up against the stage, and a few scattered drunks, flaked out at various distances back from the action. By the time you're past the half way line, there's nobody back there at all. Way too cold out there even for the drunks.

Actually that's not accurate. It's more like two people in front of the stage at one side, one person at the other side, and half a hat and a shoelace a hundred meters from the stage. In other words, almost totally deserted and covered in snow.

Some parts of Canada are breathtakingly beautiful, with the most familiar glamor shots of Canada being winter scenes devoid of people. Which is a true depiction. 99.999% of the time, 99.999% of the land mass of Canada has exactly zero humans standing on it. The obvious cold makes it a far from perfect environment for the human animal. The percentage of land area of Canada that is occasionally warm enough for humans to go outside without being bundled up in sleeping sacks is a mere 3.8% of the total.

Canada's the second biggest country by area and shares the longest land border in the world with its extrovert southern neighbor. The fact that almost none of the population of the USA is scrunched up along its northern border is further evidence supporting the initial observation about the environmental comfort of Canada.

Canada is a surprisingly peaceful country. Surprising because they can't even agree on a language to speak. But it wasn't always that way, as a succession of home grown terrorist groups tried for years to force a separation of state from state on the basis of language. Between 1963 and 1970, a series of groups, all of whose names could be formed be rearranging seven fridge magnets depicting the words Liberation, Front, Army, Revolutionary, Quebec, Popular, and Movement, engaged in robberies, bombings, kidnappings, a plane hijacking and murder. Their popularity diminished as Canadians realized it was far more entertaining to work out their differences in a more organized manner, still popular today. Uniformed teams face off on ice rinks, throw down their gloves and protective helmets and punch the snot out of each other while referees, who can be distinguished from escaped cartoon prisoners by the orientation of the stripes on their uniforms, only get involved when the punch drunk players are too exhausted or concussed to continue to fight effectively.

Canada's mostly famous for a trailer park and the boys who live there but other famous and not so famous Canadians comprise a truly diverse roster of inventors.

Chris Haney and Scott Abbott invented Trivial Pursuit in 1979, and Earl W Bascom co-invented the side-delivery chute, as well as inventing the reverse-opening side-delivery chute, the hornless bronc saddle, one-hand bareback rigging, and high-cut chaps. P L Robertson invented the Robertson screw and R L Jeremy invented the Jeremy screw. Ringette is a snowflake version of ice hockey, which utilizes a soft rubber ring instead of a puck, and outlaws body checks. It was invented by Sam Jacks who also invented boxette, boxing with no physical contact, and roulette, a game with no rules.

Charles Fenerty invented the wood pulp process for making paper, although it was an accidental discovery, as Fenerty was actually researching a method of pulping neighborhood children who refused to stop playing ringette in the street outside his house. The popularity of ringette diminished rapidly following the disappearance of Fenerty's neighbors' children.

Had Thomas Carroll, Gerald Bull and Joseph-Armand Bombardier collaborated, they may well have invented a self-propelled-G5-howitzer-combine-harvester-snowmobile-Iraqi-supergun, and not many people know that "The Real McCoy" was a Canadian invention that facilitated the lubrication of machinery.

Ringette was not the most famous game invented by a Canadian, and nor was five-pin bowling, which doesn't really warrant a credit as it's no more of an actual game invention than the pastimes children make up when left alone for an afternoon with an assortment of old junk including a ball, some sticks, matches, a hammer, a soggy pornographic magazine and a pair of pliers. The most famous game invented by a Canadian was basketball, the brainwave of James Naismith, a six foot eleven inch (2.11m) native of Ontario. Naismith is not related to Mike Nesmith's mother, who invented Mistake Out, aka Liquid Paper, or to Romy White or Michele Weinberger who invented Post-Its.

The other Canadian inventor of note is Harry Wasylyk who invented the disposable green polyethylene garbage bag in 1950 and lived long enough to see his status transition from "brilliantly clever guy" to "idiot that's trying to destroy the planet".

Much more significant and useful than most Canadian inventors is The Great Randi, one of the world's foremost opponents of charlatans and snake oil. In 1964 the James Randi

Educational Foundation (JREF) offered a cash prize, which increased over time to one million U.S. dollars, for anyone who could demonstrate supernatural or paranormal ability. Over a thousand people applied to try to take the prize, but unsurprisingly, they all failed. The One Million Dollar Paranormal Challenge was discontinued in 2015 when Randi retired.

By many measures, Canada's a great place for people to live, largely because of the things humans have created to make it that way. Which is why there's been a lot in this section about the people of Canada. But for the purposes of judging planet earth as a perfect human environment, the question is, how often is it comfortable to walk around outside with almost no clothes on? The answer for most of Canada is never, and for those living in a really tiny portion, hardly ever.

About a mile and a half south of where most Canadians live is the USA, a country that boasts of being the greatest democracy the world's ever seen while simultaneously granting corporations all the benefits (with none of the responsibilities) of being a human citizen, whilst denying a fair shake of the stick to anyone not lucky enough to be born rich and white. The USA is a country that bans slavery yet still finds a way to enrich wealthy prison owners by incarcerating poor black people through discriminatory laws and bail systems. A country that, at the time of this writing, has a morally bankrupt, malignant narcissist, racist puppet of a foreign crime boss in the White House, and where the rule of law is on the verge of collapse. There is a depth of resilience and decency in the citizenry that still affords the USA a chance of becoming a better democracy, rather than devolving into a full on criminal kleptocracy, and lesser republics would have collapsed before now. A brief amount of time will reveal which way the USA goes.

Climatically, the USA is a mixed bag. The top third's a lot like where all the Canadians live. Visually beautiful in all seasons, but physically uncomfortable a lot of the time. Eight and a half million people live in New York City despite the fact that it can get unbearably hot in the summer, and bitterly cold in the winter. An argument could be made that that the number of people who choose to live there is proof that it must be a good place to live. And New York is a great place. No argument on that. But it's a great place despite the climate, not because of it.

Southern California is a great place to live because of the climate. In the past it didn't have enough water, but that's been sort of fixed, at least for now. California has the highest and lowest points in the contiguous United States and they're only about 84 miles (135km) apart. California also has earthquakes, which is related to the previous fact, and a wildfire season, which isn't. Alaska's already out of the running as a suitable habitat for humans on account of its latitude, but it also has volcanoes, as does Hawaii, which is a shame as it has mostly perfect weather.

The southern border of the USA looks like it's been drawn by a committee that couldn't agree on anything. The western part that separates Mexico from California, Arizona and New Mexico, was drawn by the guy with the ruler who wouldn't lend it to the guy who was having a heart attack as he scribbled the line from El Paso to the Gulf of Mexico. The real reason the border's squiggly for the entire southern border of Texas is that it's a river, called the Rio Grande. Which isn't nearly as grand as it once was with irrigation demands leaving it at less than 20% of its former size. In fact, there have been times when its been so dry that a sand bar has formed across its mouth. Anybody who's woken up after a big night on Dos Equis and Patron knows exactly how the Rio Grande must've felt.

Were one to build a wall between Texas and Mexico, where would it be? On the Texas side, thus ceding the construction zone and all of the river to Mexico? On the Mexican side, thus requiring an act of war to annex the required dirt, and the river? (Or should that be a further act of war, as it's less than 200 years since Texas was acquired using the same method.) Maybe all the way along the middle of the river? Degree of difficulty 9.8. Also, according to Wikipedia, the official river border measurement ranges from 889 miles (1,431km) to 1,248 miles (2,008km), depending on how the river is measured. If it can't even be accurately measured, how the hell do you build a wall along it?

Another thing that's difficult to measure is the exact altitude of Mexico City, although we do know that it's the highest city in North America (and the oldest), and we also know that it's sinking on account of being built atop an underground lake which is being emptied in order to slake the thirst of the inhabitants. The thing that makes Mexico City really old is that it's built on the ruins of the great Aztec city of Tenochtitlán.

The Aztecs weren't the first Mexicans. That title probably belongs to the Olmecs (1400-300BC), who sculpted colossal heads and worshipped a god that was part human and part jaguar. They're the ones who started the blood sacrifice rituals in Mexico, a tradition that's been practiced off and on ever since, and continues to this day. Mostly by drug cartels. The Olmecs were serious hardasses as they sacrificed infants and babies, something the cartels only indulge in when they really need to teach someone a lesson.

The Olmecs and the Mayans may have thought they had cool-sounding names, but the Aztecs and Zapotecs, by taking the extremes of the alphabet and strapping them in front of tec, nailed them to the wall on that. Aztec and Zapotec are still brilliant words even today so we can only imagine how awesome they sounded back then. It's unsurprising that the Zapotec developed the first writing system in the Americas. They were good with words.

The Zapotec (600BC - 800AD) also did their share of blood sacrificing to all manner of deities, who represented rain, light, maize, spring and anything else that needed a bit of a spiritual hurry up. They apparently believed that they came from the earth or caves except for their ruling elite who said they came from supernatural beings who lived in the clouds. Modern day descendants of the Zapotec call themselves Be'ena' Za'a, which means cloud people.

The Aztecs were the undisputed champs of ritual blood sacrifice, which may indicate that individuals with a sociopathic lack of empathy were more common back then. Although seeing the gleeful faces in a crowd watching a young woman being publicly beaten for the crime of immodesty in Aceh province, Indonesia, certainly challenges that idea.

Aztecs, of course, had not been exposed to ringette. They'd have definitely sacrificed anyone who even suggested such a tame game. Instead they played a ball game known as tlachtli in which the losers were sacrificed to the gods.

Aztec priests (its always priests) would hold their sacrificial victim down, cut out her still-beating heart with a ritual blade decorated with the faces of the gods for which the sacrificial heart was intended, and cast it into a fire. Between 10,000 and 250,000 victims a year were sacrificed. Montezuma II, was the individual all-time ritual sacrifice champ, once overseeing the slaughter of 12,000 victims in a single day. It's a good thing they had religion to give them a moral code or who knows what they might have got up to.

Today the dominant religion in Mexico is Catholicism. This may or may not have been a positive development depending on whether you prefer the idea of having your children murdered or sodomized. Those priests, eh? Always up to something.

Mexican children get their Christmas presents on the 6th of January, to celebrate the day they believe that the three wise men arrived with gifts for the baby they each apparently thought might have been theirs. The fact that they arrived together and seemed to know each other, and that they'd apparently all cuckolded Joseph, though possibly not at the same time, suggests that they may have had some sort of grooming gang affiliation.

The weather in Mexico's really good in general and many parts are absolutely wonderful. The Tropic of Cancer runs through the middle, meaning it's half temperate and half tropical, with further variations due to altitude and other geographical features. If the geography and climate of the whole planet was like Mexico a few billion people would enjoy a much better quality of life.

Except for the few hundred thousand who'd be gunned down in the streets. If you combined the more heavily armed areas of Mexico and the Philippines, you'd have a place that resembled The Purge episode of Rick and Morty.

Central America

Central America consists of seven countries: Guatemala Belize, El Salvador, Honduras, Nicaragua, Costa Rica, and Panama.

Guatemala is most well-known in New Zealand for the following sentence. "You're not in Guatemala now, Dr Ropata." The most famous line in the history of New Zealand television is from Shortland Street, a medical soap opera still going strong after 27 years and more than six and a half thousand episodes.

Belize is the only Central American country where English is the official language although mixtures of Creole, Spanish, Garifuna and Mayan are also common. The mythical creatures of Belize are also a mash-up, both scary and reassuringly kind of dumb. There's a 3-foot tall, evil dwarf called El Duende who has no thumbs and dwells in the forest ready to punish any children who kill animals. Nice thought, but opposable thumbs might have made the little critter seem like more of a threat. There's also a creature that's a lot like a sasquatch or Big Foot, who likes the taste of human flesh but has no knees and has its feet on backwards. Belize sounds almost perfect, with a lovely central American climate and the scariest creatures are comically harmless, so long as you don't venture too far off the path in the Cockscomb Basin Wildlife sanctuary, the world's only jaguar reserve. That's where the wild things really are.

If one were to think about exports from El Salvador, coffee and sugar may spring to mind. Yet El Salvador generates more export income from electrical capacitors than from either of those commodities, and twice as much from t-shirts as both of them combined. The capital of El Salvador is San Salvador, a fact that has led to momentary confusion and the demise of many quiz show contestants.

Honduras has a festival to celebrate the fishnado, not to be confused with Sharknado, the movie, or fish tacos, the delicious snack. Father José Manuel de Jesus Subirana was a Spanish priest who arrived in Honduras in 1855. According to legend, Father Subirana prayed for three days and three nights asking God for a miracle to feed the poor. God apparently tired of listening to the priest's nagging prayer and a deluge of tasty fish tacos rained from the sky.

This has allegedly recurred every year, although it's only been celebrated with a festival since 1998 when residents of Yoro, Honduras initiated the Festival de Lluvia de Peces (rain of fish), sometimes known as the Aguacero de Pescado (downpour of fishes), to celebrate the phenomenon.

The date of the festival, which includes a parade and carnival, is variable (thus complicating the efforts of skeptics to record the event), and loosely coincides with the first major rainfall in May or June. It is improbably surmised that a waterspout originates in the Atlantic Ocean, which is about 200km (140 miles) away, and causes a single fishnado each year. It's alternately speculated that the fish may be flushed from a nearby river after a heavy deluge and into a drainage system that deposits the fish in the town centre.

Neither theory gets anywhere near explaining how the fish get cooked and sauced and deposited into the tacos. Truly a miracle. Nice one, Father Subirana. It is not known if Father Subirana was ever accused of being a pedophile, but feeding the poor would have provided an almost impermeable cover for such priestly hijinks back then.

Also popular in Honduras are the legends of El Cadejo, a sort of devil-inspired bad-dog, good-dog thing, that helps or hurts travelers, and La Llorona, the ghost of a woman who lost her children and who spends eternity crying whilst looking for them in a river, and who is thankfully not real, as she is said to bring serious misfortune on all who hear her.

Nicaragua is world famous mostly for the Iran–Contra scandal in which the Reagan administration committed so many serious crimes, at such high levels of government, that most of the criminals involved either went unpunished or were pardoned or promoted.

Despite an embargo banning the sales of weapons to Iran, senior administration officials secretly conspired to do exactly that.

Israel was the middle man, and while it does seem incongruous that Israel would supply weapons to Iran, Iran's wish list for neighborhood annihilation was at that time topped by the Sunni controlled states of Iraq, Kuwait and Saudi Arabia, with the Jews of Israel being consigned to the back burner, probably because of Israel's nukes, which their surrounding Muslim neighbors know they'll only use as a last resort. They also know that they definitely would use them if necessary, so their neighbors know they're better off trying to show their god they're on his side by killing as many of the wrong type of Muslims as possible. The wrong type of Muslim is any type of Muslim other than a Shia, if you're a Shia, or any type of Muslim other than a Sunni, if you're a Sunni. The same also applies to other Muslim sub-cults.

The Iran-Contra story is like the premise for a spy thriller. Seven American hostages are being held in Lebanon by Hezbollah. Iran can probably convince Hezbollah to release the hostages, but they'd really like a whole bunch of American weaponry, especially ammo and parts, because they've got a lot of older American equipment left over from the time when Iran was an ally, aka puppet state of the USA. So Israel sells Iran the weapons, and America resupplies Israel who pays America with funds given to them by America.

Oliver North then steps in to suggest diverting (or stealing) some of those funds to give to the Contras, who are trying to overthrow the Sandinistas, the relatively popular government of Nicaragua, who are in the process of enforcing the will of the majority of the people who, after a fifty year diet of

Somozas, have become heartily sick of them, as the only variation had been an occasional change of topping.

The Sandinistas, on account of their socialist inclination, were unpopular with the US government who were responsible for installing the all-Somoza diet in the first place. (Coincidentally, American dissatisfaction with Iran and Nicaragua both began after the ousting of dictators who had been installed by America.)

Although fourteen high ranking officials were indicted, including the Secretary of Defense, all eleven of those convicted were pardoned by George H W Bush, who had been Vice President at the time of the crimes.

Justice must not only be done, it must be seen to be done. And then undone, as soon as the spotlight recedes.

One of the still famous Iran-Contra criminals is Oliver North who has continued his life's work as a shit-stain on planet earth by providing toxic commentary to Fox News and briefly becoming president of the NRA. North revoked his Catholic affiliation in order to join an evangelical church, for reasons of political expedience, and has a net worth in excess of five million dollars. That's only half as much as Wayne LaPierre, but Ollie was fairly confident that he'd find a way to accumulate big bucks, or big rubles as they mostly are, from a slush fund like the NRA.

Costa Rica's national flower is the orchid. Orchid comes from the Greek word orchis, meaning testicle and was named by Pedanius Dioscorides, a Greek doctor who often worked naked in the summer months. After accidentally dropping the tuber in his lap, Dioscorides noted that the tuber he was examining looked very much like his left nut.

Panama is famous for the Panama Canal, the Panama Hat and the Panama Papers. Panama Papers are not a type of paper made from a machine like Charles Fenerty's Child pulping machine, rather they are documents containing evidence of thousands of illegal dealings of many obscenely wealthy criminals.

All the countries of Central America share a common feature with Mexico. The Spanish Conquistadors brought them the gift of Catholicism, which included a Spanish Inquisition level of cruelty and forced subservience for the adults, and a scourge of pedophilia that is continuing to wreak havoc on thousands of children to this day.

South America

Brazil is the big daddy of South America, having about half the land area and almost half the people. It's hardly surprising they're so good at football with a population of more than 200 million to choose from. Most of them speak Portuguese, which means it's the biggest lusophone nation in the world. The reason they speak Portuguese is that Brazil was claimed for the Portuguese empire by Pedro Álvares Cabral on the 22nd of

April, 1500, when he landed there, apparently by mistake, whilst attempting to sail to India.

It seems more than a little fortuitous that an explorer can successfully lay claim to one of the largest countries in the world as a result of poor navigation skills, but the rules were loose back then, as pretty much all discoveries were the result of poor navigation, one way or another. One way or another is explorer jargon for a navigational decision based on a coin toss.

In 2009 Brazil banned tanning beds. They have not attempted to ban the string bikini, the Brazilian thong, or the Brazilian, so their efforts at protecting Brazilian skin from dangerous UV ray exposure seem somewhat ambivalent.

Brazilian authorities are firmer with respect to protecting Brazilians from deadly snake bites, as civilians are banned from landing on Snake Island, which lies about 20 miles off the coast of Sao Paulo. Why anybody would want to set foot on an island with between one and five snakes per square meter is a mystery. To put it into perspective, that's about eighty to one hundred times the concentration of snakes that were on the plane with Samuel L Jackson.

In 2011 Stjnio de Cassio Zequi, a urologist in Sao Paulo, published a study which found that 35 per cent of men from rural Brazil have had sex with an animal. 59 per cent of the zoophiles in the study did the dirty deed for one to five years, while 21 per cent did so for more than five years. The subjects reported a variety of frequencies for their depraved activities, ranging from monthly to daily and the target species included mares, cows, pigs and chickens, among other animals.

A total of 492 men, between 18 and 80 years old, took part in the study, which found that men who had sex with animals during their lifetimes were twice as likely to develop cancer of the penis as those that restricted their sexual encounters to humans.

73.6% of the population of Brazil is Catholic. When considered together with the above study, that may indicate that just under half of rural Catholic Brazilian men have had sex with an animal. The percentage of Catholic priests who have had sex with Brazilian children is a secret locked away in the vaults of the Vatican, but is widely believed to be a much larger number.

There have been no similar studies done for men from rural Greece, Afghanistan or Australia, so it is not known whether these Brazilian statistics should be considered a good or a bad thing.

Argentina is almost as good at football as Brazil. But not quite. It's got far fewer people to choose from (44m to 208m), and the climate is way worse. Argentina stretches all the way from the middle of the continent right down to the bottom. The capital of the Argentinian part of Terra Del Fuego is Ushuaia, the southern most city in the world, according to Argentina. About 57,000 people live there. The reason is a mystery. Average top temperature in the warmest month is 10°C (50°F), and the sun is visible on average less than 4 hours a day. On top of that it's really windy, of course, being close to Cape Horn and the most notoriously dangerous piece of ocean in the world.

The Tango was invented in the slaughterhouse district of Buenos Aires around the end of the 19th century, and was a popular form of dance-based foreplay for many years. The Last Tango was performed in Paris in 1972, much to the annoyance of all Argentinians who had, up to that time, successfully exploited the dance not only for personal seduction purposes, but also in their tourism and prostitution industries.

An effort was made, ten years later, to revive the dance at an event scheduled for the Gaiety Dance Hall in the town of Stanley in the Falkland Islands, but Maggie Thatcher was informed about the potential insurrection and declared that no Latino vertical folk dancing would be taking place on any British protectorate while she was still alive, so the British armed forces launched an attack.

Most commentators agreed that the British attack had as much to do with England's humiliating run of World Cup failures, and especially Argentina's win in 1978, as anything else. Although England won the battle of the Falklands in 1982, their loss in the war that really counts was rammed home in 1986, when Argentina lifted their second World Cup, a sting no doubt intensified in the brains of English football hooligans by thoughts of Germany's 4 victories, and Brazil's 5.

The name Argentina comes from the Latin word argentum, meaning silver, which reflected the belief of the European settlers/invaders/conquerors/exploiters that the country was chock full of the precious metal. It may help to process their attitude toward this new land by considering the mentality of a person who would name an adopted child, Freshmeat.

Argentina is famous for meat consumption, producing almost 4 million tons per year. That's a ton of meat for every ten people. They also have the world's highest sales of laxatives and haemorrhoid cream. Argentina is the only country in the world where surgeons perform emergency c-sections of the bowel. Often following the Buenos Aires' Meaty Feast Championship.

Argentina is also known for a fascination with dead bodies. In 1971, the ex-president of Argentina, Juan Perón, had the embalmed body of Evita exhumed from its grave in Italy, where it had been secreted after much Shakespearean malfeasance and skullduggery, and flown to Spain, where he lived with his new wife Isabelita. Evita's body lay in their dining room, until Juan stopped crying for her for the last time in 1974. There's a great deal more to this story, which is well worth the time, but is far beyond the scope of this book.

Australia is generally recognized as the world champion of changing heads of government, but at the end of 2001, Argentina grabbed the record with 5 Presidents in 10 days. Australian politicians have, for the last twenty years, been debating term limit legislation that would allow them to reclaim the title they believe is rightfully theirs, but it hasn't been brought to a vote as they've been too busy organizing coups against various Prime Ministers.

Chile is basically the beach of South America on the west side. If it were an adolescent at high school, it would be called a long tall streak of weasel's piss, or, if you were any longer I wouldn't wait for you. It's the longest, narrowest country in the world. If that weren't enough Chile also has a mountain range, the Andes, which has more than 2,000 active volcanoes and runs the whole length of the country. It squeezes the population into an even narrower stretch of land, between sea and potential death by lava bomb. Which means that Chileans live in a long straight line, much like Canadians.

The Andes aren't the only uninhabitable part of Chile as there's also the Atacama Desert which is as dry as dry gets. Parts of the Atacama have not had any rain at all, as far as anybody knows, at least since the beginning of observations and record keeping.

For many years Augusto Pinochet made even the nicest, most habitable parts of Chile a risky and unpleasant place to live, as, with the support of the CIA, the "Chicago Boys" (a group of Chilean economists who studied at the University of Chicago under free-market guru Milton Friedman), and Henry

Kissinger, he kidnapped, tortured and killed tens of thousands of Chilean citizens during the 1970s and 80s.

Summary

For warm blooded animals there are too many months of cold weather pretty much everywhere north of Santa Barbara, or south of Bolivia. If you also discount places with too many crocodiles or alligators or sandflies or mosquitos or that are too prone to hurricanes or tornadoes, places that are too mountainous, too wet, or too dry, you end up with the proportion of the land mass of the Americas that qualifies as the sort of place that's perfect for human habitation. And that's probably still being a little generous because a place perfectly designed for human habitation wouldn't have any extreme weather events that cause flooding, power outages, trees falling on houses, houses falling on cars, lightning strikes on golfers and the like.

In 2018, Hurricane Florence caused massive flooding in the Carolinas and it wasn't just water that damaged everything. It was sewage, overflow from pig shit reservoirs, coal ash, and all manner of chemical nastiness that can take years or longer to be properly cleaned up. But even a proper clean up is no help to the people already killed or who acquired permanent illnesses from the contamination.

America - Proportion of land in the Goldilocks zone - 14%.

EUROPE

Britain is nice, in parts. London can be a huge amount of fun, but if you were going to live there you'd want to be rich enough to be able to get away to somewhere warm and sunny for maybe nine months of each year. Or spend almost all of your time inside buildings that effectively insulate you from the weather outside. Which means it's not a great natural environment for human habitation. Iceland and Scandinavia can be dismissed for the same reason, but more emphatically.

And so to the continent. The northern part has unpleasant weather for most months of every year, and although there are some great cities, they are, like London, great despite the weather, not because of it. Paris is spectacular and wonderful in different ways in every season, but the cold grey gloom of winter brings most residents down to a state of near depression by the time spring comes around to rescue their mental health.

Belgium's the country you drive through when you're on your way to somewhere else. Apart from the magnificent Spa-Francorchamps circuit and the movie, In Bruges, there's really not much reason for Belgium to exist.

Germany's main claims to fame are beer and Nazis, but you can find more than enough of both of those things pretty much anywhere you go. More than enough beer means waking up with a hangover and beer in the fridge, and more than enough Nazis means one.

Switzerland and Austria are lovely to look at, like cute and cuddly bears, but mountains are also like grizzly bears in that if you spend too much time with them you end up dead. Or in a mind-numbingly stupid movie riding a galloping horse off a hundred-foot-high cliff, if you're Leonardo DiCaprio.

The best bits of Europe are the bits around the Mediterranean. A fairly large chunk of Spain, France and Italy and all the way round to Greece, are pretty damn close to perfection when it comes to a place suitable for human habitation. Except for winter, which is too long and too cold, or when the Mistral blasts down the Rhone Valley for days on end, which has been known to plunge some people into permanent insanity.

It has long been said that it was insanity that caused Van Gogh to cut off his ear but that's not what really happened. Van Gogh was probably teetering a little toward cabin fever after being housebound for three days by the Mistral, as one evening he was reported to have declared, "Fuck it. I don't give a shit what the fucking wind's like tomorrow, I'm going painting."

True to his word, Vincent set out first thing in the morning. The Mistral wasn't as strong as it had been, but it was still blowing. With some difficulty, Van Gogh managed to set up his table and stool, but it should have been obvious even to a madman that a painting on an easel was never going to stay put. Nevertheless, he persisted, holding the edge of the canvas with one hand as he sat down to get to work. But then, needing two hands to open a tube of paint, he briefly released the canvas, which immediately took off and set a course for the Mediterranean via the Camargue, and may well have gone all the way had a bush not interrupted its flight.

Van Gogh retrieved the canvas and turned back, blinking into the head wind as he fought his way toward his easel. He was lucky to have his eyes open at the very moment the wind lifted the blade of a palette knife and hurled it toward him like a spinning ninja attack star. Van Gogh was not particularly agile, and managed to move his head just enough to avoid the knife slamming into his eye, but not enough to avoid it completely. So he was now faced with having to retrieve his ear, the palette knife and the canvas, which had flown even further away, as he'd released it in shock at the moment of his de-auriclation.

For reasons unknown, Van Gogh wrapped his ear in paper and delivered it to a brothel that he and Gauguin frequented, before he arrived back at his digs in a far worse frame of mind than when he'd left. It has been said that he never laughed again.

From this moment his mental condition spiraled downward and despite, or probably because of, the homeopathic ministrations of Dr Paul Gachet, Vincent was pretty much doomed to heal himself or die. Van Gogh's death was recorded at 1:30am on the 29th of July, 1890, thirty hours after a bullet from a 7mm Lefaucheux revolver entered his chest. Whether the fatal shot was self-administered or the accidental result of horseplay with a couple of drunk youths in cowboy costumes is the subject of much disagreement among historians.

A belief in homeopathy wasn't the only problem afflicting Dr Gachet. Van Gogh described the doctor's mental condition as "sicker than I am, I think, or shall we say just as much". Van Gogh wrote in a letter to his brother Theo, "I have seen Dr. Gachet, who made the impression on me of being rather eccentric, but his experience as a doctor must keep him balanced while fighting the nervous trouble from which he certainly seems to me to be suffering at least as seriously as I."

The summer of 2018 continued a trend of being the hottest on record across Europe, causing flamingos to luxuriate in the pink of life, and, along with other tropical birds in wildlife reserves in Britain, to lay eggs, something they'd not done for fifteen years.

It wouldn't be too much of a stretch to consider this information with respect to the sexual behavior of Britons, as it ties in with research that indicates that most British babies born in the last forty years were conceived in Malaga,

Benidorm, Magaluf or Ibiza. The recent trend of warmer summers may change this.

Europe's a smallish continent covering about 2% of the Earth's surface and 6.8% of the land area. There are about fifty countries in Europe, the biggest one being Russia, even though most of it's in Asia, and of all the dividing lines between continents, the one between Europe and Asia looks the most arbitrary.

The European end of Russia is easily the wealthiest end, and Moscow is easily the wealthiest city. In fact, all the people who control pretty much all the wealth in Russia have at least one address in Moscow. If they decided to socialize, they'd comfortably fit inside one house. One large room in fact.

After the fall of communism, the most ruthless men in Russia managed to steal almost all the assets of the Russian state in an impressively short period of time, and it all ended up in the coffers of about twenty-two mob bosses.

Russian men are famous for being some of the most dedicated guzzlers of alcohol on the planet. The two most common reasons for drinking are fun and abject despair. A country in which the military, and all branches of law enforcement, report to the boss of bosses is never going to be fun for most people. So the overwhelming majority drink for the second reason.

During the Cold War it was reported that the Russian Air Force would have struggled to get more than about twelve percent of its aircraft off the ground, such was the shortage of hydraulic fluids after ground crew discovered that they contained alcohol. People who drink for fun and partying purposes don't generally opt for mechanical lubricants as their preferred tipple, and they also don't tend to work in places where such fluids are abundant. There are no official casualty statistics published by the Russian Air Force with respect to brake fluid ingestion, but in the overall population one in five Russian men die of alcohol related causes.

Drunkenness may also be a contributing factor in Russia's seriously declining population levels. The Governor of Ulyanovsk, declared September the 12th to be the Day of Conception. Citizens can have part or all of the day off to try and conceive a child, and women who give birth closest to June 12, Russia's National Day, receive prizes such as a UAZ-Patriot crossover vehicle, the Ulyanovsk region's version of an old Lada Niva chassis with SsangYong lookalike bodywork. Second prize is a home appliance. The region's birth rate often triples in the month of June.

In 2012 it was suggested that young married couples of Ulyanovsk may be gifted air tickets and a weekend in a cheap hotel in Malaga, Benidorm or Magaluf, to encourage copulation for the population, but the funds that had been appropriated for the project were embezzled by a young hoodlum thought to be the grandson of a distant cousin of mob boss Semion Mogilevich, so the project was abandoned without investigation.

Over 30% of children in Russia are born with diseases or physical or mental defects attributable to air pollution or contaminated drinking water due to heavy industry, weapons factories, alcoholic parents, traffic emissions, and the UAZ-Patriot assembly plant in Ulyanovsk. Russian oligarchs have shown no interest in environmental protection legislation, as there's no money in it for them. American oligarchs are following their lead and are beginning to have some major successes in their efforts to destroy the previous good work done by the EPA.

Europe - Proportion of land in the Goldilocks zone - 18%.

AFRICA

Africa is the birthplace of all humanity, so it would seem reasonable to assume that big chunks of it must be Goldilocks Zones. Which turns out to be the case, apart from a large expanse of desert in the north, called the Sahara, which is as big as the United States.

Africa has spent most of the last century trying to get its shit together as a result of being colonized and then decolonized. This is never a smooth process as there'll always be a bunch of grifters looking for the opportunity to fleece the coffers of any country in a state of transition. That should not be construed as a dig at Africans, as the best examples of this type of grifter are Vladimir Putin and his Russian mafia colleagues. Also known as oligarchs. Another example, with greed, dishonesty and ambition equal to that of the Russian mob, but with skills not yet so well honed, is the Trump administration.

When one considers that most colonial governments spent a large part of their time helping themselves to as much as they could carry away from the local economies, it's not surprising to find that there are many African governments that are still not terrifically good at governing for the benefit of the citizenry. It seems to be an unfortunate fact that people who are the most driven by the desire to enrich themselves at the expense of the population, are also the best at getting themselves into a position to do so.

Nigeria is well known for having a large number of Princes who have been taken advantage of, but who nevertheless still have just a few million dollars available to them. Often this money is very difficult for them to access, in which case it may require being transferred into the bank account of a random stranger with a gmail address in a wealthy western country.

Widows and widowers in their forties or fifties usually have the most suitable bank accounts for a Nigerian Princes' money. Sometimes the Prince is deceased but his loyal servant still has the ability to access the account, provided a few conditions are met. The loyal servant may need to travel to a different town to access the money. Or he may need to pay off a debt to a lawyer in order to free up the cash. Or he may need a few thousand transferred into a kick-starter account to get things rolling.

In Nigeria internet fraud is known as a 419, which is probably a reference to a statute or criminal code or similar. The most successful 419 in Nigeria's history was massive, in fact the third largest banking scam of all time up until recently. Only the job Nick Leeson did on Barings Bank, and Qusay Hussein's looting of the Iraqi Central Bank were bigger. They're all starting to look a bit like small beans as we find out more about the 2008 sub-prime economic collapse, Deutsche Bank, 1MDB, Bank of Cyprus, Danske Bank (200 billion Euros laundered so far) or anything to do with Russian oligarchs, but they were big at the time and the Nigerian one is still very impressive for the sheer audacity and scale of the underlying lie.

Emmanuel Nwude was the Nigerian 419 champion between 1995 and 1998 when he committed the largest fraud in Nigerian history by selling an airport to a Brazilian bank called Banco Noroeste for $242 million. The most impressive part of the scam was that the airport didn't exist. Nwude is described in Wikipedia as a Nigerian advance-fee fraud artist, although maestro or champ would also work.

The scam utilized the standard 419 ingredients of impersonating someone else, in this case, Paul Ogwuma, a governor of the Central Bank of Nigeria (CBN), and appealing to the mark's greed, by offering Banco Noroeste executive Nelson Sakaguchi a ten-million-dollar bung on the deal. Nwude and his co-conspirators were eventually exposed when Banco Noroeste was in the process of being acquired by Banco Santander and the Santander auditor discovered that half of the bank's capital was inexplicably parked in the Cayman Islands.

Nwude and his five accomplices were arrested, and following a complicated series of trials involving bribery, kidnapping of witnesses and bomb threats, Nwude was eventually sentenced in 2005 to five concurrent five-year sentences, a $10 million fine and forfeiture of his assets.

Following his release from prison less than a year later, in 2006, Nwude further confirmed his status as a fraud artiste by successfully suing for the return of his assets which he claimed to have acquired prior to the scam. By 2016 he'd been rewarded with $167 million for his efforts, but then something akin to OJ Simpson Syndrome must have caused a malfunction in his brain as he managed to get himself sent back to prison for totally unrelated crimes.

A land dispute in the town of Ukpo in the Dunukofia area escalated when two hundred men invaded the Abagana community, killing four policemen and the security guard at a construction site. The Anambra state government accused Nwude of being behind the attack and he was arrested and charged with 27 offences including murder and terrorism.

Arraigned on different fraud charges, Nwude applied for bail, which was denied by the judge, because he was already serving a jail term. Nwude appealed on the basis that there was no evidence placed before the court that he was actually serving a jail sentence. He argued that if he'd been in jail he couldn't have committed the crimes he was charged with.

He is being held at Awka prison at the time of writing, but how long he'll remain incarcerated is anybody's guess. Nigerian bookmakers are giving odds on the method of Nwude's liberation, offering even money on judicial bribery, prison level coercion, kidnapping and armed breakout. There are also side bets available on numbers of accomplices and whether or not there will be any helicopters or armored vehicles involved.

Nwude's airport sale was not the first 419 scam Nigeria had ever seen, but it was so impressive that it's often credited with being the driving force behind the popularity of the advance fee fraud industry in Nigeria.

How this whole thing will end is anybody's guess, but whatever happens let's just all pray, very, very hard, that Steven Spielberg doesn't acquire the movie rights and cast Tom Hanks as Emmanuel Nwude.

The country directly to the south of Nigeria is Cameroon, which should not be confused with macaroon, a sweet meringue-based confection of French origin, made with egg white, icing sugar, sugar, ground almond, and, most importantly, food coloring, as the macaroon's distinctive feature is that they come in a huge assortment of colors. The macaroon, or macaron, as the French spell it, should also not be confused with Macron, which is a President rather than a confection.

McRon, which is the shortened version of McRonald as in McRonald McDonald, is the jovial clown mascot for the McDonald family restaurant chain in Scotland, but has nothing to do with France or Africa or the American Ronald McDonald.

Cameroon often produces a very good football team, as does France.

African Nations cooperate through the African Union which has recently benefitted from a major sponsorship deal recognizing African achievements in long distance running and vibrant markets and is headquartered in Adidas Alibaba, the capital of Ethiopia, formerly known as Addis Ababa before the naming rights deal.

Africa covers 6% of Earth's total surface area and 20% of the land area. The equator runs right through the middle of Africa, and the continent extends beyond the tropics in both directions. A great deal of the country has a reasonably nice climate. There's also a lot of desert, as in most of the northern half. It's a hot and dry continent overall with more than 60% of it being drylands and deserts.

Africa - Proportion of land in the Goldilocks zone - 14%.

Proportion of land in the Goldilocks zone, that's not dangerous because of nasty humans and other dangerous animals - 3.2%.

THE MIDDLE EAST

According to myth and legend, God concentrated all his efforts for making the world a great place for human life on just one tiny part of the Middle East. The three major religions that came about as a result of God's fiddling in that small un-godforsaken desert have created an area that only the adventurous or those with an insanely strong religious affiliation would want to go anywhere near. There are also those who have the misfortune of having been born there, but who have yet to discover the concept of not-gonna-stay-in-a-shithole-under-the-thumbs-of-religious-fanatics, a concept often abbreviated to refugee.

Some refugees don't fully understand the concept and therefore take the religious fanatic disease along with them, which of course solves nothing for anybody, and just makes things worse everywhere.

The local inhabitants of the Middle East have been involved in killing each other for religious reasons, ever since their religions were invented.

There are many places of beauty in the Middle East, and a pleasant enough climate (albeit with a bit of a water shortage), to make it fall easily into the Goldilocks Zone, but the humans that live there make a peaceful and pleasant existence pretty much out of the question.

The Middle East -

Proportion of land in the Goldilocks Zone - 35%

    Goldilocks Zone minus Killing Zone - 0%

ASIA

Asia's so big and diverse that it's almost pointless to think of it as a single entity. But for some reasons we do. The Middle East is treated separately in the previous section, even though it's usually identified as part of the Asian continent. Turkey, Israel, Saudi Arabia, Yemen, India, Thailand, Malaysia, Indonesia, Japan, Korea, China, Mongolia, Kazakhstan, Russia and Siberia have enough different cultures to fill a Star Wars theme bar with costumes representing a dozen galaxies.

The 'Stans, northern China, Mongolia and the Siberian end of Russia comprise the northern 65% of Asia. Like the Middle East, most people wouldn't want to live there, albeit for different reasons, and only the most curious and intrepid would be interested in even a brief visit.

Ulaanbaatar is the capital of Mongolia. It started as a movable monastery, changing locations 28 times before settling permanently at the present location. Now with a population of over a million it's not surprising that they've decided that rolling up the yurts and moving on is logistically more hassle than it's worth. As Genghis Kahn was reported to have said, "Most of the time we move on we end up somewhere even shittier than where we just left. Fuck it, let's just stay here for a bit." Ulaanbaatar is the coldest national capital in the world, where the average temperature is -1°C (30°F).

Mongolia's so cold that Mongolian horsemen inadvertently invented, or more correctly discovered, how to make ice cream without any form of artificial refrigeration. Mongolian horsemen used animal intestines as containers for all manner of fluids, including cream. After a good gallop across the Gobi in winter they'd often find that their cream, having been vigorously shaken as it froze, had turned into ice cream, albeit not the sweet version we're now familiar with. That came later after Marco Polo returned to Italy in 1925 with the Mongolian horsemen's recipe in his pocket. Actually it was more of a technique than a recipe, as, at that time, there was only one ingredient.

The addition of sugar and sweet, crushed fruits to make the delicacy we all love today is credited to Bojack Horseman, a retired American sitcom star who is also, coincidentally, a distant relative of a Mongolian Horseman family. Whilst holidaying in Italy, Bojack was enjoying a bowl of Marco Polo gelato when another tourist, mistaking Bojack for an actual horse, proffered a few sugar lumps toward his mouth. When Bojack turned his head, his long nose bumped the cubes into the bowl of unsweetened ice cream in front of him. He then proceeded to consume the sugar and frozen cream together, and declared the dish to be delicious and absolutely the best thing since sliced bread. Sliced bread was accidentally invented by

Attila the Hun and had, up to that point, been the best thing for a very long time.

When Bojack returned to California he opened an ice cream stand on the corner of Fairfax and Wilshire offering 41 flavors of sweetened iced creams. The stand was briefly successful before the concept was widely copied and it closed down some years before Biggie Smalls was shot and killed nearby. Rumors that Bojack Horseman was in some way involved are totally unfounded, although the full story may never be known. As a counterpoint, Suge Knight was not in any way involved with adding sugar to ice cream, although it's not unreasonable to think that Suge might have a sweet tooth given that his childhood nickname was Sugar Bear.

South of the too cold zone, Asia gets a lot more enticing. It has some of the most spectacular and beautiful places on earth including many that have become tourist destinations.

Tourist destination is a term that makes a lot of people cringe, and it's certainly true that tourists can destroy the essence of a place. For example, any Spanish town that has "restaurants" with display signs for "fish and chips". Another example is Kuta in Bali. Previously beautiful areas are often littered with towns that have succumbed to the tourist dollar. But the thing about tourist destinations that aren't based on theme parks or great cities or ancient ruins, is that they were once, before the tourists arrived, stunningly beautiful, always warm enough for a human body to be naturally comfortable, and therefore easy qualifiers as places in the Goldilocks Zone.

Indonesia is made up of 17,508 islands. 11,500 of them are uninhabited by humans. This is all the evidence you need to establish that the human race is nowhere near as clever as most humans think we are. These thousands of vacant islands are not only beautiful but they're so absolutely in the Goldilocks Zone, that it's astonishing that they remain unoccupied while millions of people live in places like Siberia, Alaska, Mongolia, Kazakhstan and on remote islands such as Falkland and Shetland. Tom Hanks and his volleyball would have quickly perished in any of those places, and by so doing would have saved a lot of us an hour or two of wasted time.

The first European tourist to visit Indonesia was Marco Polo, in 1292. Polo was perceived as some kind of pale skinned god, and locals soon began calling his name in a form of ritual repetition, usually in conjunction with a display of synchronized swimming or other water-based activity.

It's a tradition that continues to this day and Marco Polo can often be heard as a repetitive chant in both resort and private pools all around the world. With two notable exceptions.

The Marco Polo mantra has not been heard in Crimea since 2004, when Semion Mogilevich was roused from an afternoon nap he was enjoying in the penthouse suite of a luxury hotel in Yalta. Even for non-sociopaths not trying to sleep, the sound of an enthusiastic game of Marco Polo can be infuriating.

Mogilevich asked his bag man what the fuck was going on and told him to "take care of it". There has been speculation since as to his intention, and whether his instruction was properly carried out, but Mogilevich's boys took care of it Putin-style. They dragged six tweens from the pool, marched them to the beach and executed them in front of a few hundred shocked sunbathers.

On a sunny Sunday afternoon in Baghdad in 1998, Uday and Qusay decided to go out and get some new girls. Young men all over the world talk this way, but when Uday and Qusay said it, they meant it literally. They were known for walking into nightclubs, taking women by the arm and dragging them out. If a woman's boyfriend objected, he was killed. Such were the joys of living under the rule of Saddam.

Back to that Sunday afternoon. Uday and Qusay walked into the pool area of the Baghdad Hilton and looked around. They saw a couple of attractive woman sunning themselves by the pool and walked over to talk to them. At the Baghdad Hilton, it was the practice to talk to women before dragging them off, just in case they were representatives, or related to representatives, of an important foreign government. An afternoon kidnap and rape mission was easier without the hassle of setting off a diplomatic incident. As they walked over to speak to the women, Uday was annoyed by a loud game of Marco Polo that started up in the pool right next to them. He turned, pulled out a pearl-handled, gold-plated 45 Magnum and shot one of the kids in the head. Mayhem and screaming ensued, and the women the Hussein boys were about to hit on were up and gone before they could be stopped. The brothers were so annoyed that they shot another eight swimmers to make themselves feel better.

It has been claimed that the person who ratted out Saddam by providing American forces with the location of his spider hole was the great uncle of one of the children killed by Uday and Qusay at the Baghdad Hilton pool.

Despite the demise of the Husseins, the aural pollution of the Marco Polo abomination has not been heard in Iraq since that day. Some say it's no longer an acceptable game to play as a sign of respect for the deceased, but most adults understand that the threat of summary execution is a good way of keeping the lid on one of the more annoying noises known to mankind, a noise that falls into the same category as chainsaws in suburbia.

In Taipei, the capital of Taiwan, there's a market called Snake Alley that serves some very exotic foods including snake blood, deer penis wine, and turtle blood and meat.

Taiwan is also partly responsible, along with Japan, for the least exciting, but possibly most consumed, food in the world - ramen noodles. Momofuku Ando was born of Japanese parents in Taiwan at a time when Taiwan was under Japanese control. Following a move to Japan and a couple of failed businesses, Momofuku made his name at the age of 48 when he introduced Chikin Ramen to the world in 1958. Not content to rest on his noodles, Fuku introduced an even blander version, Cup Noodles, in 1972, when he was 61. Thankfully Fuku died at the age of 96, without coming up with an even less appetizing version of the humble noodle, although The Instant Ramen Museum (aka Cupnoodles Museum) in Ikeda, Osaka does credit Fuku with a third invention. Space Ramen, which was announced in 2005, was the result of his decades-long effort to invent a ramen that could be eaten in space.

From the Cup Noodles Museum website - "Along with applying various techniques for eating in weightless environments, Space Ramen is based on the hot oil instant drying method that Momofuku invented in 1958. With Space Ramen, Momofuku's creative thinking transcended the bounds of earth to contribute to creating food that people can eat even in space."

Enrolment applications for the NASA astronaut school declined dramatically in the late 2000s, although it's not known if the announcement of the invention of Space Ramen had anything to do with that.

For people who can't make it to Ikeda, there is a second Cupnoodles Museum in Yokohama.

The Taipei Times published an article on Saturday the 27th of November, 2004 with the headline - In honor of the Little Black People - and a subhead - "The Saisiyat tribe of Hsinchu and Miaoli will perform a solemn rite this weekend to commemorate a race of people that they exterminated."

This is a true story.

The "Ritual of the Little Black People" involves drinking, singing and dancing and has been performed for over a hundred years to bring good harvests, ward off bad luck and keep alive the spirit of a race of people who are said to have preceded all others in Taiwan. The pygmies (which sounds like a pejorative but is the correct term according to the official reference material) reputedly taught the Saisiyat tribe how to farm their land, but after a session of non-ritual drinking and singing a fight broke out and the Saisiyat killed all the pygmies.

Asia covers about 8.7% of the Earth's total surface area or 30% of the land and is home to roughly 60% of the world's population.

Asia - Proportion of land in the Goldilocks Zone - 18%.

ANTIPODES

Australia is the name usually given to the continent down under. Australia doesn't include the islands off to the east, although NZed and Oz have a lot more in common than Kazakhstan and Japan, which are both part of Asia. The differences are mostly apparent in accents and at sporting events.

Australia's a bit like Canada in that humans don't live in most of it. They're mainly gathered along the eastern and southern edge, a bit like Canadians along their southern border. This is the closest part of Australia to New Zealand, although that's not generally thought of as the reason for the eastern concentration. The population density of Australia is less than one hundredth of the population density of the UK. And it always will be, as the great big middle part of Australia would be almost as difficult to colonize as Mars. The only thing in the outback conducive to human survival is air. On Mars if you didn't need to breath you'd freeze to death on your first night, so you'd definitely last longer in the Australian outback, but not by more than a few days.

There are ten deserts in Australia, but without GPS there'd be no way of knowing that you'd crossed from one to another. Australian deserts are like bread sandwiches in that regard. The only thing separating the bread is more bread.

Just because it's a place you wouldn't want to live doesn't mean the outback isn't fun for some, and there are plenty of special events held out there including horse races, camel races, pumpkin rolling, gem festivals and B & S balls (where B & S means Bachelors & Spinsters or Beer & Sex, and ball means a mock-formal, dust-covered, all-you-can-drink orgy). And there's the Australian version of Burning Man, the Deniliquin Ute Muster.

The Deniliquin Ute Muster occurs when a few thousand delinquents drive into the outback in cars that have truck backs instead of a back seat, and spend a few days getting drunk and behaving badly. A gathering of utes may sound like My Cousin Vinnie trying to organize a militia, but a ute is to Australia what a tru-uck, (being the phonetic spelling of the two-syllable variant of the word in common use in the southern states) is to America. America has the Ford F-150 and the Chevy Silverado. Australia's equivalents are imaginatively called the Falcon Ute and the Holden Ute. For those unfamiliar with Australian vehicles, they look more like a Chevy El Camino than a tru-uck.

As well as excessive drinking, the Deni Ute Muster offers activities such as driving utes around dusty paddocks and driving utes around muddy paddocks. The best utes have large metal structures on the front which are designed for killing kangaroos and large metal structures on the back which are designed to make the ute look more macho. Utes are often adorned with banks of large spotlights, four to six very tall radio aerials, and large flags, perhaps six or eight of them. Water trucks are brought in to convert dusty paddocks to muddy paddocks for events that are better with mud, such as wrestling, and naked-fat-drunk-man-running-falling-and-sliding-in-the-mud, which isn't listed on the official event program, but is one of the most common and popular events nonetheless. After the mud slide fat event, the lads get dressed, usually in stubbies (short shorts) and t-shirts or black wife-beaters adorned with witty drinking slogans, beer labels, Ford or Holden logos, or words such as Titties, Beer and Fishing.

The Delinquent Ute Muster will eventually become a gathering for old vehicles, as the production of Aussie utes ended in October 2017 when the last Holden Ute rolled off the GM production line. The last Falcon Ute was built by Ford in July 2016. Australian utes are now being replaced by American style trucks, mostly made in Asia, which are suddenly being bought by everybody, especially the version with a back seat and back doors as well as a truck back.

In Hands on a Hardbody, a documentary about a car dealership endurance contest in which desperate punters try to keep their hands on a tru-uck longer than anybody else, one of the contestants is asked, "What's the best thing about owning a truck?" After a long pause the good ole boy answered that it was good to be able to help friends move house. He was then asked about the jawbreaker in his mouth, and he said it was good because eating jawbreakers meant he got to go to the dentist more often.

Large numbers of people seem to have decided that they prefer hard-riding, evil-handling, rattly trucks, over far more refined regular cars. The reason is a mystery. People who haven't gone all the way to trucksville, often settle for an SUV instead. These don't have a truck back, and generally tend to be a lot nicer to drive, but they still tip over without waiting to be asked, and whilst they're much easier for parents to load children into car seats, they're also much more likely to result in the demise of said children, as death and serious injuries are many times more common in accidents when vehicles invert.

One of the astounding things about Australia is that the second biggest city, Melbourne, is built in a place with pretty much the shittiest climate in the whole continent, if you don't count the desert. Or Tasmania. Melbourne sits at the top of a south facing bay that funnels icy Antarctic winds straight up Melbourne's jacksie. Strangely, Melbourne's also prone to summer temperatures that can reach over 40°C (105°F). Melbourne's often said to have four seasons in one day, which makes deciding what to wear on any given morning a complete pain in the ass. Often it makes sense to pack a bag with alternate seasonal clothing, even if you're just popping out for a soy-skinny-latte or an avocado toast brunch, or going for a spin around the park or the laneways on your fixie.

Some early settlers got back in their boats and left the generally wonderful climate of Sydney, and sailed south towards Antarctica to settle the island of Tasmania, a place with a great deal of visual beauty, but a climate arguably worse than Melbourne's. Maybe not that much worse. But anyway. Holy crap. You've found a lovely warm place with a brilliant harbor, some of the most perfect beaches and most abundant flora and fauna in the world and you say, fuck this, let's head towards the South Pole and live down that way instead.

In Queensland, if you don't mow your lawn for two weeks you're a mango farmer. If you drink as much as a professional sportsman you can pass out anywhere and there's no chance of freezing to death, regardless of the season. In Queensland you can walk into any body of water, wave your arms around for a bit and go home with armloads of delicious seafood. There's also the chance that that the seafood, or perhaps a croc, will go home with a delicious feed of you, but that'd be rarer than a sober teenager at Schoolies week in Surfers Paradise.

Brisbane's nowhere near as cold as Melbourne in the winter (a frost is almost unheard of) and summer temperatures rarely rise above 30°C (~86°F). Why it's not as popular, or populated, as Melbourne is a mystery. Also a mystery is why Melbourne quite often gets a nod as one of the most livable cities in the world. Whatever that means. It's possible that such polls or surveys or whatever they are, are organized by polar bears or Swedes because Scandinavian cities often rate highly in such things.

Boris Yeltsin is arguably the most well known booze enthusiast among heads of state, but it was former Australian Prime Minister, Bob Hawke who claimed a world record by sculling two and a half pints of beer in eleven seconds. Unlike Boris, Bob was never discovered in his undies outside the White House late at night trying to hail a cab to go for a pizza, and never got close to triggering a gunfight between Russians and American Secret Service agents in the basement of Blair House. Yeltsin had many famous drinking adventures, but he never held an official world record, although his performances in Washington, given that they happened on two consecutive nights, is a record unlikely to be bettered, and should probably be more widely recognized. An annual "Boozing for Boris" weekend of drinking events, including hourly vodka shots, and eating pizza in your undies would be appropriate. Although in Deniliquin, it would simply be called Tuesday. Or Wednesday.

Australians respect a drinking man regardless of profession, but none more so than sports heroes whose post-match drunken misadventures and humiliations are so common as to barely warrant a column inch unless they involve public defecation, large quantities of class A drugs and one or two dead hookers.

And it's not only post-match drinking events that find their way into Aussie folklore, sometimes a decent pre-match session is also deemed laudable.

David Boon was an Australian cricketer who is celebrated mostly for having consumed 52 cans of Victoria Bitter, or VB, on a flight between Sydney and London in 1989, a feat highly enough regarded for the Qantas pilot to have announced it over the intercom as the plane began its descent into Heathrow. The announcement was received with a hearty round of applause and cheering, so it's safe to conclude that most of the passengers were Australians.

Boon, even though he was a professional sportsman, was the same shape as a beer keg, and reportedly had been drinking during his trip from Perth to Melbourne, then from Melbourne to Sydney, where he joined the team for the flight to London. It's unknown how many beers he enjoyed during those first two legs but he was reported to have nailed three quick schooners in the lounge at Sydney airport, and also to have partaken of two or three cleansers during the Singapore stopover, although under the official rules of Australian long distance drinking, those weren't included in Boon's total, as only airborne drinks on official flight legs may be counted.

A Prime Minister and a professional cricketer who are most famous for their beer drinking prowess is a pretty good indication of what many Australian citizens aspire to. Although they'll happily settle for a big night on the piss at the Twin

Towns Resort and Casino culminating in a modest win on the pokies. If they've caught a few fish in the morning, and watched a footy match in the afternoon, so much the better.

While many people are critical of the way Australia changes Prime Ministers more often than pommies change their undies, it can't be denied that Australia's a hell of a lot better place to live for the vast majority of citizens than anywhere that keeps a leader for more than a term or two.

Likewise, there are critics of New Zealand's form of government which is by proportional representation. Their reasoning is that they hate the way that politicians can't get anything done. Given the freedom, prosperity and general well-being of the vast majority of New Zealanders, when compared to governments under "strong" or "strong man" leadership, it's hard to see that as a bad thing.

New Zealand has a female Prime Minister who isn't married, and who had to take maternity leave shortly after taking office. This was loudly criticized, but it occurred without the sky falling, or in fact anything much happening, which is how the system generally works.

New Zealand women were the first women in the world to achieve the right to vote in 1893, 9 years before most of Australia in 1902, 27 years before the USA in 1920, and 35 years before the UK in 1928.

Many people from Europe and America are under the impression that the weather's really good in New Zealand. The truth is there's a half a chance of the weather being good in December and April and a reasonable chance of it being good in January, February and March. But those lovely, balmy summer nights where you can sit outside wearing no more than a t-shirt and shorts are rare. Single figures. Although recent years have been warming up and changing that.

Antipodes - Proportion of land in the Goldilocks Zone - 7.9%

ANTARCTICA

Antarctica is a continent-sized desert of the polar variety. It's totally unsuited to human habitation although there are a few bloody-minded souls who've set up some of the ugliest trailer parks in the world down there. When they come to their senses and go home, the legacy they leave behind will mostly be a rubbish dump. And mountains of frozen turds, like on Everest.

People go down there mostly to carry out scientific research but also to see if there's anything worth plundering. Like oil. The industry plan for extracting Antarctic oil involves burning all the oil we currently have, thereby clearing away the ice and snow that's in the way of the final extraction.

Antarctica -   Proportion of land in the Goldilocks Zone - 0%

AFTER THOUGHTS

According to people of faith, planet earth was created specifically for human habitation. Everything on the planet that's not us, was put here for us, to utilize.

Part of the reason we may think humans are so significant is because pretty much everywhere we go we see lots of other humans. Most cows think the same thing. Wherever they are, there are lots of other cows. If a cow dozes off and the herd moves to the far side of the paddock, she'll waste no time in wandering slowly across to join them, thus restoring normality. A world consisting mostly of cows.

Regardless of the anecdotal experience of humans, most of the planet isn't occupied by humans, and of all life forms on earth, humans, all seven and a half billion of us, make up an astonishingly tiny proportion. By weight, we make up just 0.01% or 1/10,000th of all earthly living things, according to "The biomass distribution on Earth", an article published in PNAS, one of the world's most-cited, and wittily named, scientific journals, in May of 2018.

Plants make up 82% of life on earth. There are 7,500 plants per person. Most of them aren't tasty or nutritious, but they do produce oxygen which is a good thing.

The second largest component of all life on earth is bacteria, at 13%. Even though we've known for some time that there are millions, or billions of bacteria living on and inside every one of us, it'll come as a surprise to most to learn that on a pound for pound basis, bacteria actually outweigh us, and by a huge margin. For every kilo of human on the planet, there are 1,300 kilos of bacteria. One can only guess how many football fields that would cover if one could spread bacteria like butter. Somewhere between one and a thousand probably. There's also a baseball stadium or two of fungus (2% of total) for every human.

But back to the football field. Rugby league is played with thirteen players on each team. So if there were a hundred rugby league teams lined up, two teams across, fifty teams deep, on one end of the field, and a single person facing them on the other, that's the proportion of bacteria to human that the creator decided was about right.

After plants, bacteria and fungus, just 3% of the biomass is everything else. All the fish in the sea, birds, animals, insects, puppies etc.

But we humans are doing our best to fix that. Experts estimate that we have, so far, halved the number of plants on the planet, and destroyed over 80% of the wild animals. Almost half the animals on earth have been lost in the last 50 years.

A few thousand years back the proportion of all human-affiliated animals on the planet was tiny. Now, we humans, along with our livestock, outnumber all wild mammals and birds by almost twenty to one.

According to Ricky Gervais the collective noun for big game hunters is cunts. Can't argue with that. Except to add psychopathic to the title. And murderous. Psychopathic murderous cunts. The thing that makes them so much worse than other types of killers, is that they do it for fun. And the more beautiful their victim, the greater their pleasure. They're happy to pay extra for rarity, for the thrill of killing the most endangered of species. And they'd like nothing better than to be able to brag to their deplorable friends that they personally killed the last living white rhino. Could anything be more psychotic than the killing of beautiful creatures for enjoyment?

Also, it's well past time we stopped using the term "big game." A large caliber bullet, suddenly and without warning, slamming into your head or body is about as far from fun and games as anything could be for a sentient creature.

Hunters are working towards reducing biodiversity to the point where there'll only be cows, sheep, pigs and chickens left for them to kill. If they really have to kill animals to get their jollies, why not transition now, and start killing cows instead of beautiful, free, endangered animals?

Oh, that's right, it's because they're cunts. They make out that it's somehow sporting to shoot an innocently grazing giraffe, but I've yet to hear an explanation of the specific difference in sportiness between driving along in a Land Rover, stopping and shooting a giraffe, and driving along in a Land Rover, stopping and shooting a sheep. One of them is classified as sport, a big game, and the other is the sort of thing that will get you arrested, and possibly sent for psychiatric analysis. Unless you're the farmer who owns the sheep.

None of which is meant to excuse the cruel treatment of livestock in which most us are complicit, but just as soon as the scientists perfect a method for making delicious tasting burgers, steaks, bacon and eggs out of things that aren't animals, there'll be no reason for us to keep abusing and killing them. Obviously we'll have to eat most of them to restore a more natural balance of species and to avoid an Indian-style sacred cow problem, but that wouldn't take long.

In the same way, it's obvious that we'll eventually have to rely on renewable energy for all our power requirements, so why not make a big effort to get on with it, rather than burning all the rest of the oil and coal right now with the inherent risk of killing the planet? Oh, that's right, it's because people make a lot of money out of it, and the most powerful of those people are assholes. The sort of assholes that enjoy killing things.

Hopefully the scientists will get the artificial meat thing to happen very soon along with a way to remove the psychopath gene from the human gene pool, and we may be able to begin to peacefully co-exist with the planet's other residents, rather than killing them all. And each other.

The state of the planet before we started our annihilation program indicates that the creator spent more than 99.99% of his time creating stuff other than mankind, most of which none of us will ever come into contact with. It could be imagined that the creator was the greatest procrastinator of all time with access to an internet of all things, and kept on getting sidetracked on every little piece of research to such an extent that what might have been a tightly focused piece of work, a perfect creation for mankind with a majority of it being a perfectly formed Goldilocks Zone, ended up as a hodge-podge of all sorts of stupid stuff of peripheral and questionable value. Sort of like this book.

Humans, especially those over the age of about forty or so, generally feel healthier and happier when the air is warm and the sun comes out every day. Obviously such conditions are the right conditions for humans to live in.

But most of the planet isn't like that. Even the Goldilocks Zones have a fair bit of crappy weather. Including wind.

Wind is easily the worst of all individual weather conditions. By a long way. Cold is next. Followed by rain. A combination of all three is almost unbearably horrible. The other significant elements of weather are temperature, sunshine and humidity. Humidity's not usually as bad as wind, rain and cold. But sometimes it is. Humidity sucks when it's really hot, but it's even worse when it's cold, creating damp walls, mold and disease.

Sunshine and temperature are the good guys. Even when you choose to sit in the shade, it still feels better when you can see the sun's shining. Extended periods of overcast, drizzly, damp skies have been known to make people feel genuinely suicidal.

On the other hand, too much direct sunshine unfortunately leads to burnt skin and sometimes cancer, thereby killing you, even though you're living in a place that makes you want to stay alive. A larger volume of atmosphere that blocked the harmful UV rays would be a much better design, and given that it's so easy to imagine, the current situation can only be regarded as deliberate malevolence on the part of a creator.

Latitude, altitude, proximity to large bodies of water, prevailing winds, and ocean currents all affect local weather. Which explains why no two places feel quite the same.

A true Goldilocks Zone would be sunny and mostly calm all day every day, with a bit of breeze and rain from 1am to 3am to keep the system running. That would provide plenty of healthy plants including shade trees on which to hang a hammock for an afternoon nap.

If such perfection were to get too boring, there'd be other places to go for a bit of variety. Mountains to ski on, or windy beaches for windsurfing. Even if you chose to go to a cold grey eastern European city in winter for a bit of perverse variety, it would be so much better arriving home from your holiday to a Goldilocks Zone, rather than doing it the other way round, that is arriving home to spend the next fifty weeks in a relatively unpleasant environment.

CONCLUSION

The Goldilocks Zone, in astronomical terms, is the position in space that a planet must occupy in order to capture enough heat and light from the star it orbits to support life as we know it. The most basic requirement is the maintenance of a consistent temperature between zero and one hundred degrees Celsius, being the range in which water is water, rather than ice or steam. We wouldn't do well with ice in our veins, or steam, and neither would plants or anything else we may find useful on a planet.

Astronomers, who call the Goldilocks Zone the Circumstellar Habitable Zone, or CHZ, when formality requires, currently think that there are about 11 billion earth-sized planets orbiting in the CHZs of sun-like stars in the Milky Way. And countless more beyond. Which makes any thoughts about this planet being the apple of the creator's eye extremely narcissistic.

There's also a smaller Goldilocks Zone on the surface of planet earth. Applying the minimum requirement (0-100°C), the north and south poles are out. And so is anywhere within driving distance of the circles, Arctic or Antarctic. But the comfort zone for most humans is much narrower than CHZ minimum requirements, it's more like a daytime outdoor temperature between 18 and 27°C (65-80°F), with nights a few degrees cooler for a comfortable sleep.

Not many places on earth provide anything close to this on a consistent basis. Rather than planet earth being a perfect place designed for humans, it's really a place that has a small number of pretty good parts, but mostly it's not so good, requiring solid buildings and artificial heat sources to make them habitable.

As previously mentioned, it's said by some that New York has to be rated as a great place to live on account of the millions who choose to live there. With the improvements made by humans it is a great place. For those who can afford it. Without improvements, it'd probably still be pretty good in summer. But in winter you'd freeze to death.

If population density was a relevant indicator, then you could argue that the best place on earth is that prison in the Philippines that's so densely populated you have to sleep standing up, but it's more likely a contender for least desirable place on earth to live, along with the Shetland and Falkland Islands, parts of Syria, and Luton.

Some like it cold

As promised in the introduction, here's the bit that takes into account the strange fact that some people prefer to wear many layers of clothes at all times.

For those who prefer it colder, the percentage of planet earth in your personal Goldilocks Zone actually decreases. This is because the greater the latitude, or distance from the equator, the shorter the planet's circumference at that point.

The 45th parallel is half way between the equator and the pole. In the northern hemisphere, the 45th parallel runs through the United States just south of the Canadian border, through the south of France, the north of Italy, Romania, Crimea, Kazakhstan, China, and Mongolia. In the southern hemisphere the 45th parallel doesn't cross much land at all, just Chile and Argentina where they're quite skinny, and the South Island of New Zealand, which is also slim.

One mile of latitude at the equator, amounts to a total surface area of 25,000 square miles, or 64,000 square kilometers, whereas at the 45th parallel one mile of latitude amounts to less than 18,000 square miles or 45,000 square kilometers.

So even for those whose perceived Goldilocks Zone is colder, the overall conclusion, which is that there's not much of it, is even more valid. And the further you get from the equator, the smaller your zone becomes.

The suitability of planet earth for human habitation is a given.

But how much of it is really, really excellent for that purpose? If we apply the Goldilocks principle to the whole planet, just how much is there?

Water, meaning mostly oceans (which, as previously discussed, are a much more stable environment for fish than the atmosphere is for humans), covers 71% of the surface area. So that's out.

According to The Physics Factbook, earth's land surface can be divided into five different types:

Land covered by snow and ice - 20%

Mountains - 20%

Arid land - 20%

Land with no topsoil - 10%

Fertile land - 30%

In other words, the land that's possible for humans to survive on is 30% of 29%, or just 8.7% of the surface area of the planet.

But that's without having made a deduction for the Red Zones, the Black Zones, the Windy Zones, the Code Red Zones or the Killing Zones, or the fact that most of that 8.7% lies outside the Goldilocks Zone as far as comfortable temperatures are concerned.

When the calculations are all done, less than 3.4% of the surface area of planet earth qualifies as being an excellent place for humans to live.

Given how much of this planet is not a perfect place for human habitation one can only conclude that we were an accessory, a side hustle, an afterthought, almost an accident of nature perhaps.

The notion that this planet was solely designed and created for the benefit of mankind is not in any way supported by looking at what is actually here.

Even though the Goldilocks Zones of Planet Earth are nearly perfect places for us to live, so good that they might have almost been designed for us, the argument for a creator stumbles when one considers that it should have been just as easy to create a planet with a bigger proportion of Goldilocks Zone. Would 50% be too much to ask? An omnipotent god could theoretically make one with 100%.

The planet we live on has a Goldilocks Zone of just 3.4%.

Not a good effort.

Not Very Intelligent Design.

What sort of designer would create a universe, including billions of galaxies, trillions of stars, and a solar system with one small planet for all of humanity, and then make 96.6% of that tiny planet either unpleasant or absolutely uninhabitable? A mysterious one for sure. One that might be worth having a good think about. Preferably while staring up at the stars on a warm clear night with a fine glass of wine.

If for some reason the sheer awesomeness of the stars above makes you think there must be a creator, that there must be something special about planet earth, consider that in the part of the milky way you're looking at, there are billions more earth-like planets up there and any number of them just might have areas of Goldilocks Zone, with millions or billions of inhabitants, and given the numbers, chances are some of them are sitting there right now, looking up into their night skies, looking right back at ya.

The End

To read more by Neel Ingman, go to

neelingman.com

Thanks for reading

Reviews are the best way to help other readers find books they'll enjoy.

A review that's brief, just a sentence or two, will let other readers know what you liked about the book, and why you think they may like it too.

So if you enjoyed this book please leave a review or at least a rating at Amazon.com or Goodreads.com or anywhere else that you can.

And PLEASE DO IT RIGHT NOW before you forget (you know you will).

If you'd like to be notified of new books by Neel Ingman please sign up to the mailing list at neelingman.com

Cheers, Neel

Printed in Great Britain
by Amazon